ESSEX SURVIVALS

THE GUILDHALL, THAXTED

ESSEX SURVIVALS
WITH SPECIAL ATTENTION TO ESSEX SMUGGLERS

BY

FRED ROE, R.I., R.B.C.

AUTHOR OF
"ANCIENT COFFERS AND CUPBOARDS" "OLD OAK FURNITURE" ETC.

METHUEN & CO. LTD.
36 ESSEX STREET W.C.
LONDON

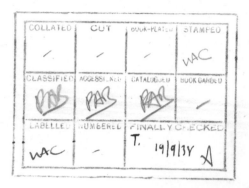
First Published in 1929

 ~~675N~~

PRINTED IN GREAT BRITAIN

PREFACE

THAT the present work is not intended to be a guide-book will account for the fact that hackneyed features of the more palatial show-places in Essex find but little mention therein. Regarded, as that county has been for many years, as a species of backwater only to be approached through the eastern fringe of the metropolis, it is extraordinary how many of its antiquities and curiosities have been preserved, which under other conditions would have probably long ago been improved (?) out of existence. To those who have Essex blood in their veins the county is often little less than a religion. But its bibliography can hardly be called an extensive one, and a goodly proportion of the books about it which have been issued in recent years are more or less resurrection dishes, compiled directly from earlier publications.

Among the treatises consulted during the composing of the present volume mention may be made of the Inventory issued by the Royal Commission on Historical Monuments : *Transactions of the Essex Archæological Society* ; *Social England*, edited by Traill & Mann ; *The Essex Review ;* the Rev. J. H. Stamp's *Lectures on the Parish and Abbey Church of Waltham Abbey ; The History of Dagenham*, by the Rev. J. P. Shawcross ; *London's Forest*, by Percival J. S. Perceval ; the London Survey Committee's monograph on *Eastbury Manor House ;* Thomas Wright's *History and Topography of Essex ;* and, of course, Morant's pioneer work on the county.

For personal courtesy shown to me I am indebted among others to the Rev. J. W. Eisdell, R.D., Rector of Orsett 1916–1928 ; the Rev. T. H. Curling, R.D., Vicar of Halstead ; Mrs. Hutley, of Doreward's Hall, Bocking ; Mr. F. Brand, of Ilford ; Messrs. Walford Bros., the topographical booksellers, themselves members of an old Essex family ; and, for valued assistance, to my son, Mr. F. Gordon Roe ; and Mr. Arthur G. Wright, late curator of the Corporation Museum, Colchester, who has since passed beyond.

FRED ROE

September 1929

CONTENTS

LIST OF ILLUSTRATIONS

xi

THE MARTELLO TOWER,
WALTON-ON-THE-NAZE

Hold the book with its back on a
the front cover down, then the back, ho
while you open a few leaves at the bacl
so on, alternately opening back and f
sections till you reach the centre of t
three times and you will obtain th

Never force the back

If the volume is opened
place you will likely break the
leaves.

A little precaution will add

Misty Moon Marsh

CHAPTER I

MISTY MOON MARSH

WHERE is Misty Moon Marsh?
It lies somewhere in that 'recondite region' bounded by the Stour and Lower Hope Reach on the Thames. Anything more specific than that I dare not say.

At the quiet village which overhangs the winding creek intersecting the salt marshes nothing seems doing, for the tide is out and does not 'serve'. A few boats and craft of the humbler sort lie canted on the mud bordering the attenuated ribbon of water, tributaries of which form mooring-places for two or three house-barges. The approach to these habitations is invariably in the form of a quaint little gangway, terminating in a drawbridge some four feet in

1

length. Farther on the tributary squeezes out into a sort of ditch or moat, replete with disused kettles and broken pans. On an eminence near by the square tower of the church dominates the sun-drenched village street, with its tumbled group of picturesque sixteenth-century houses. And always about here the longshoremen lounge, with furtive, cautious eyes. There is a hospitable-looking big-beamed old inn, full of quaint nooks and unexpected corners, where homely fare is served by a comely damsel, exhibiting a liberal development of shapely arm. The ale is cool and good, and one ' modest quencher ' leads to another before we emerge into the blazing street—and again encounter the same watchful loungers, who do not appear to have shifted their attitudes.

How does the place earn a living ? Some years ago a popular Limerick was invented on the wonders of the Pelican, and I think that the last line of that clever doggerel applies with great pertinence to that quiet, red-roofed settlement bordering on Misty Moon Marsh.

Beyond the creek and stretching out interminably beneath the river-wall that skirts it lies the marsh, shimmering and vibrating in the heat like a mirage seen through a veil of vapour. A few ruminating cattle and hoarse, soaring sea-gulls are almost the only living things in sight. Myriads of insects hum out a monotonous cadence. Stranded on the mud in the distance is a good-sized barge with its sails clewed up, and apparently tenantless. Farther away still on the sea-wall lies the inert carcass of a wreck. From the river-wall bordering the creek some rickety wooden steps descend to the sun-fissured flats, and

BENFLEET

Fred. Roe.

rotten little timber bridges here and there traverse
the ' rhines ', as they are often called—or used to be
—in this part of the country. Near one of these
crossings, and half hidden by a tumble-down gate,
a lump resolves itself into the figure of a man, watch-
ing. He has been there for hours, and apparently
has nothing whatever to do. Evening comes on, and
the sun goes down in a stormy rent of fiery clouds.
A chill breath from across the water makes itself felt,
with a suspicion of wind-haze. But the man does
not move. The solitary village policeman has got
his uniform on, and presently starts on his customary
beat towards the point where he has to report to his
sergeant. We watch his bulky figure plodding slowly
and conscientiously into the twilight murk, while
away behind us a faint, mysterious radiance over the
higher ground indicates that the moon is rising. An
owl is hooting somewhere, and ruddy lights appear
in the windows of the inn, from whence snatches of
a bacchanalian song emerge on the opening of the
tap-room door.

The lone watcher has disappeared.

The air is getting chilly now, and we leave the
river-wall at a jog-trot, colliding unexpectedly with
a silent figure that leans against a tarred shed.

' Sorry ! ' we exclaim, adding in explication, ' It's
a fine night for a run.'

There is no immediate reply, but presently a belated
' Ay, ay ! ' is growled out distrustfully through the
growing darkness. Then, and only then, do I remember that the word ' run ' is also a time-honoured term
for a contraband venture.

The Crow Stone, Westcliff-on-Sea, marking the termination of the jurisdiction of the Conservators of the Thames

CHAPTER II

CONTRABAND

THE maritime County of Essex is shaped by its boundaries into something resembling the form of an irregular wedge, with the Port of Harwich at its extreme point. Without computing the estuaries the coastline may be reckoned as about something over one hundred miles from Harwich port on the north-east to the mouth of the River Lea on the south-west. A great part of the river frontage presents an agreeable opportunity for the exercise of ingenuity in the matter of smuggling.

Defoe, writing about the years 1724–5, declared that the one main industry from Thames mouth to Land's End was smuggling, and if this be true Essex

6

must necessarily have had a not inconsiderable share
in it. A tabulated history of the contraband traffic,
its repression, and consequent reprisals, would con-
stitute a catalogue of violent deeds, punctuated by
gallant actions and self-sacrifice, not entirely on one
side of the register. The profits arising out of the
game were enormous. It has been computed that if
only every fourth venture in the way of contraband
running was successful the promoters must have made
a good thing of it. Whether any of the hardy men
who made the run or effected the landing and were
caught in the act fared so well is another matter.
The craft which carried the cargoes were seldom captured, and if occasional losses in men and goods were
made they were merely inconsiderable items on the
debit side. Nevertheless the promoters of these
adventurous speculations did not always escape scot-
free. A case in point occurs. In the Castle Museum
at Colchester is a little round box, containing a set
of glass hydrometers about a hundred years old, each
something more than a large pea in size, and marked
with various figures. These were for the purpose of
testing the strength of the liquor that was brought
over, and were known to have been used by a Mr.
Thurston, of St. Botolph's Street, Colchester. From
his hands they passed into the possession of a Mr.
Hunwick, of Layer de la Haye, five miles south-west
of that town. Mr. Hunwick was a confirmed and
persistent smuggler, who used personally to accom-
pany convoys of his goods. His luck came to an end
at last, for while transporting a consignment one
moonless night his wagon broke down in Mill Lane
near Dedham Lock, and the gaugers, hot in pursuit,
captured the whole convoy, and every one with it,

Hunwick was tried at Chelmsford, and was lucky to get off with six months' imprisonment.

In my youth I conversed freely with a very ancient specimen of the old-time cut-and-thrust smuggler—almost the last of his race—a gnarled mariner who admitted that he had cheerfully proposed to drown

Relics of Smuggling Days, in the Castle, Colchester
1. *Lantern made out of an old whisky bottle*
2. *Case of hydrometers used at the end of the eighteenth century to test the strength of spirits*
3. *Custom House officer's ' barker ' or pocket pistol*
4. *Strike-a-light or tinder box, in the form of a flint-lock pistol*

in deep water a couple of intrepid coast-guardsmen who boarded his lugger. Discipline and the strong arm of the law prevailed against his lukewarm backers, and my aged acquaintance, a likely young fellow then, got a term of what he was wont to call ' King's Pleasure '. (This happened, he explained, in the last year of William IV.) In a more than usually strenuous struggle one of his eyes was knocked out, and it was with a solitary twinkling orb that the ancient reprobate eventually used to sit, discussing hot rum, with a superannuated customs officer in the latter part of his life. The hatchet was quite buried those days, and the two members of opposing factions were often to be found hob-nobbing in front of the fireplace of the 'Ship Ahoy'.

Old Pettifer (his name was not quite Pettifer) is gone, many years ago now, but I remember as yesterday his knotted veinous hands as he rowed along in his rotten tub of a boat, and the fire that shot out of his lone orb as he described his capture when his mates hung back cowed. 'They fellows', he vociferated, 'hadn't no pluck or we'd been clear of Brass Buttons.'

I have scant sympathy with contraband traffic, but as I recollect old Pettifer he was very honest, and desperately poor. A Suffolk man by birth, I believe, but his great and happy hunting ground—to use a poor metaphor—was the Stour rather than the Orwell. Toward the end of his life he earned a scanty living by vending hat-guards; for the crazy boat which he once rowed confiding pleasure-seekers out in went to pieces some years before its master. His age was phenomenal, and he could only be coaxed to talk with difficulty, but when wound up it was not easy to stop him. And his language when I—engrossed in his yarns—managed to steer his craft head-on to a floating buoy, was marvellous to hear.

The list of contraband goods on board his lugger when he was captured, I have to this day, snowed under somewhere. I note that it included, besides spirituous liquors, lace, silk and a jar of snuff. Old

Pettifer must have exploited a good many pairs of silk stockings in his line of business, but I doubt very much if the modern-day methods of Lady X, or Madame Z, who (beneath lengthened skirts) have been said to wear a plurality of these garments upon their shapely limbs, would ever have presented themselves to him. Beyond these lines I believe the eventful life of the old contrabandist remains unrecorded.

Fred Roe

Leigh High Street, from the Railway Bridge

The salt marshes bordering the Stour were the scenes of Pettifer's most fortunate ventures, and he and his mates must have kept H.M. executive pretty busy.

On the Thames estuary the steep pitch of Leigh Hill was one of the most trying propositions to negotiate, but there were (and still are) artful back-ways in that tumble-down old High Street, threaded so remorselessly by the railway, that rendered evasion easy and pursuit difficult.

THE TOWERS OF HADLEIGH CASTLE

In former times it was essential that a sharp look-out should be kept for the riding officers of the customs, and on certain vantage-points in such neighbourhoods as Manningtree and Mersea, and even as far inland as Halstead, there still exist many old buildings topped by high-roofed sky parlours, from which not only could the country-side be swept for traces of these vigilant officials, but warning lights could be flashed when ' safety first ' required it.   For, strange to say, most of the coast-side population, not excluding many a complaisant parson, were more or less partial to the smuggling fraternity.   A good deal of glorified sympathy for the habitual breaker of laws existed about the time when Harrison Ainsworth published his lurid romance *Jack Sheppard*, besides which there were occasional compensations in kind, to certain folks who might but conveniently did not notice too much.   ' The minions of the law ' had their hands quite full enough.   Flying Squads were as yet undreamed of, and one solitary customs officer had frequently to pit his unaided right arm against the deadly opposition of a number of desperadoes, and he sometimes paid for his intervention with his life.   For if the gauger was resolute, the ' owler ', when his blood was up, stopped at nothing.   A grim relic of such conflicts was discovered a very few years ago under the scope of my own observation.   A small-holder and proprietor of a tea-garden near Thundersley showed me a ' barker ', or pocket pistol, such as was carried by the customs officers about a hundred years since.   The man had noticed it lying half buried in the roots of a quick-set hedge some months previously, but had not taken the trouble to lift it out till my arrival.   It was a handy little weapon, the hammer partly gone, but the butt still retained a tiny square-shaped inlay of silver, on which were engraved the initials J.J.   What mystery lay behind the forfeiting of that protector ?   The country around Hadleigh was till the Crimean War alive with runners of contra-band goods.   J.J., whoever he was, may have been a trifle too daring.   A sound knock on the head was perhaps retaliation for an ill-aimed shot ; the gallant gauger went down for good and his pistol thrown into the nearest hedge.   It laid there, covered with growth, for many a long year, but has now found a resting-place in the Colchester Museum.

A discovery was made on the outskirts of Clacton-on-Sea, in the spring of 1928, which was considered with much show of probability to have some connex-ion with the lawless practisers of smuggling.   An old house called ' Treasure Holt ' was being renovated, when the workmen came upon portions of a skeleton of a man, surrounded with lime, underneath the living-room floor.   With the bones were a token inscribed ' John Wilkins, Ironmaster, 1793 ', and a solitary shoe buckle.

To quote a press notice, which also touched upon certain uncanny visitations at the house :

' The local belief is that John Wilkins surprised a party of smugglers making merry and that he was murdered and his body buried beneath the floor.'

But when force met force, and the preventives had an adequate backing, Mr. Smuggler rarely came out top-dog.   Some of these collisions must have been tremendously exciting.   I cannot refrain from quoting Barham, out of, to my mind, that best of all his legends, *The Smuggler's Leap*.

AN OLD-TIME 'LOOK-OUT',
WEST MERSEA

' None of them stopping, but shooting and popping,
And many a Custom House bullet goes slap
Through many a three-gallon tub like a tap,
    And the gin spirts out and squirts about,
And many a heart grew sad that day
That so much good liquor was thrown away.'

An excellent word-picture of the luckless termination of a ' run '.

Sometimes the encounter was less sporting and more
deadly.   S. Baring-Gould, in *Mehalah*, records that,
' On Sunken Island off Mersea the story went that a
whole boat's crew (of coast-guards) were found with
their throats cut ; they were transported thence to
the churchyard, there buried, and their boat turned
keel upwards over them.'

That most picturesque of buildings, the so-called
' Smugglers' Retreat ', formerly in High Street, Hythe,
Kent, reared its look-out unblushingly till a few years
ago.   It has now been pulled down, and one more of
these reminders of the strenuous days of smuggling
has disappeared from the county of Hops.   But there
are still a good many of these curiosities left in Essex ;
an excellent specimen, now grown round with trees,
exists at West Mersea, which must have been in existence at the time of the tragedy just related.

Fire-arms and edged weapons are very rarely used
nowadays in the contraband traffic.   The ' stuff ' is
side-tracked in artful methods which render inter-
ception and detection exceedingly difficult, especially
so since the disbanding of the coast-guard service.
And obviously the less bulk the contrabandist carries
the better.   It is a commonplace that there would not
be the slightest use in attempting to smuggle cargoes
of such material as timber.   Just so, but timber can

2

be conveniently made the hiding-place for highly taxed articles of a less bulky nature. The following method may, for aught I know, be considered antiquated by the watchful authorities and consigned to the traditions of Rip Van Winkle, but as an instance it is worth recording. Some few years before the Great War a timber-laden vessel was unloading its cargo on the wharf of a large East Anglian river-side town which shall be nameless. On the quay a solitary customs official, off duty, meditatively watched the process. The logs as they were raised by the crane dropped with rhythmical regularity upon the wharf. The operation went on for some time in a simple, even, and perfectly satisfactory manner. But something went wrong and the unexpected happened. One of the logs in transit swung round and bumped heavily against an obstacle, the end came off, and from a cavity tumbled a lot of tobacco. The rest happened quickly. The ruminating customs man, roused sharply from his lethargy, took his opportunity, and a whole bagful of interesting proceedings followed. I forget what the sentence was on the offenders, but it was adequate.

I have been asked if I have ever personally seen a smuggler caught in the act. Well, yes, certainly, but under very modern and prosaic conditions.

The scene is Parkeston Quay in pre-war days. One of the Royal Mail packets has arrived, and a short, very square-built foreigner, a typically ' Dutch built 'un', with pale traces of recent nausea upon his countenance, is being interrogated by an affable customs official. Between them is a deal table.

' Have you anything to declare, sir ? ' asks the officer, and the usual formula follows.

'Nein,' answers the bulky man with the hunched-up shoulders.

'Quite sure, sir?' queries the customs official.

'Ja, ja.'

'Will you please take off your overcoat, sir,' from the bland official, the faintest suggestion of an iron hand penetrating through his velvet-glove manner.

Protests in Dutch and broken English.

'George,' said the C.H.O. quietly, 'take off the gentleman's overcoat.'

Voluble protests, *ad lib.*

Many packets of tobacco are disclosed. The lining of the great-coat reveals a perfect armoury of contraband.

'Anything more, sir?'—blandly.

'Nein.'

'Take off the gentleman's jacket, George.'

Order promptly obeyed. More disclosures of contraband packing.

I will cut short the narration. Disrobing proceeded, and the man was unpicked until he presented the spectacle of a narrow-shouldered, under-developed creature of insignificant, not to mention scowling appearance.

'Anything more to declare, sir?'

No answer.

'Take off the gentleman's hat, George.'

Order obeyed. The headpiece, a square-topped bowler, was removed and a parcel of cigars fell out of it.

I have seldom seen so wretched an object as the descendant of Dirk Hatteraick, as he stood in the full light of his uncovered misery. On the bare table was a huge pile of accumulated contraband, mainly tobacco, taken from his clothing. Unpicked to his shirt the man's head looked too big for his attenuated trunk.

'Can I go now?' he asked when his garments were restored.

'No, sir. You must wait for the next train and go up under escort.'

What became of the miserable pariah I do not know. I have often wondered.

There are other dangers than detection and fine attending the personal smuggling of contraband, which it is unwise to ignore. Within the scope of my experience a man returning from the Continent concealed a quantity of tobacco beneath his outer clothes in much the same way as the Dutchman. He successfully passed the customs, but, on arriving at the London terminus, felt so unwell that he thought it expedient to step into a chemist's shop and ask for advice. The dealer in drugs listened to his tale with attention, and eventually informed the arrival that he exhibited all the symptoms of nicotine poisoning.

RELICS OF SMUGGLING DAYS
FROM THE NEIGHBOURHOOD OF COLCHESTER
1. BRAND TONGS. 2. SPIRIT KEG. 3. WINE
MULLER. 4. TINDER BOX

CHAPTER III

MEHALAH'S COUNTRY

IN the estuary of the Blackwater lie three large
islands, Northey, Osea, and Mersea. The greatest of these is Mersea ; and round it by Virley
Channel cluster a few tiny satellites, fissured out into
irreclaimable salt marshes, and almost useless in these
days, though once freely used by the smuggling fraternity. Unlike Canvey Island, farther south, these
three Blackwater islands have never proved an attraction to the bungalow builder, though Mersea, with its
peculiar fascinating beauty, bids fair to become a
popular spot for those who adopt the simple life.
And until Mersea is spoilt by some influx of accepted
villadom it is well-nigh impossible for readers of
Mehalah to ramble along those breeze-swept country
roads, alive with bird, wild animal and insect life,
and scan the wide-spreading vistas, without realizing
the curious spell of the district which the cleric-
author must have absorbed into his innermost soul
when officiating as rector of East Mersea. It is
somewhat of a commonplace to compare this extraordinary book to the works of R. D. Blackmore,
Thomas Hardy, R. H. Barham, or Arthur Morrison,
for pure localism, but one thing is certain ; for
brilliant fidelity and force *Mehalah* does not suffer
in comparison with the best of them. For over a century the pleasant pastures around Dedham, Flatford

23

and East Bergholt have gone by the appellation of
' Constable's Country,' and by a curious inversion
the low-lying marshes bordering on the estuaries of
the Colne and the Blackwater are now known as
' Mehalah's Country ', that fictitious personage having
usurped the nomenclature due to her creator.

Mersea Island is joined to the mainland at the
narrowest part of Pyefleet Channel by a sort of causeway known as the Strode, or Strood, near which in

Mediæval Coffer in West Mersea Church

the sixteenth century was a building called the
Church House, of which no vestige now remains.
The office of Strode-Keeper was vested in an official
whose duties were apparently to superintend the
upkeep of the said causeway. Until this connexion
was raised in recent times passage over it into the
island could only be effected during eight hours of
low water, and even now the causeway is occasionally
submerged. Once across the Strood and on the road
to East Mersea the way would be somewhat lonely,

but for the profusion of animated nature which throngs
the fields and roads and populates the hedgerows in
summer time.   The very birds grow cheeky at the
sight of a human being (some of the boldest almost
let me touch them), and above the hum of insect life
rise the plaintive cries of marshland wildfowl.   Solitary houses appear at remote distances, some timber-
framed with thatched roofs, others of red brick, their
fronts occasionally bearing seventeenth-century dates.
So sequestered are these homesteads that the Royal
Commission on Historical Monuments—comprehen-
sive as it is—takes no note of them.

Times have changed greatly since the profitable
old days of liquor running.   Towards the end of the
Great War, I and a brother artist found ourselves
at East Mersea one autumn day, with a biscuit apiece
and nothing to drink.   The sky was cloudless, and
the muttered thunder that had rolled unceasingly for
some four long years across the Channel was no longer
audible.   Some distance from the time-weathered old
church a humble licensed house, thatch-covered and
timber-built, reared its sign, and to this we repaired
with hopes.   No ! not a drop of anything that money
would buy.   There had been nothing to drink, ' soft ' or
otherwise, in the house for three days, though supplies
were expected ' to-morrow '.   We sought a cottage
that looked as if milk might be forthcoming.   Again
a failure.   Not a drop to be had.   An adjacent well
afforded possibilities.   We borrowed a cup, wound up
the bucket, and in defiance of unhealthy contingencies,
drank deep draughts of as pure a fluid as ever filtered
from a Company's main.   I mentally visualized the
anxious-faced old landlord at the inn as he would
have appeared a century or so previously, his stealthy

eye roving casually over the blue water visible beyond
Mersea flats, and his thoughts divided between a
probable moonless night and the good ship *Main
Chance* laying calmly in the offing.   For the proprietors of such ' kens ' knew better than to pay duty on
the stuff they traded in when cargoes could be run
quietly and occasionally one of the ' brass-buttons '
squared with ' palm oil '. I sighed for a friendly
contrabandist. A house of public entertainment
drained absolutely dry of food and drink would have
been inconceivable in those lean days.

On the south-east corner of Mersea Isle the
entrance to the Colne was, until the middle of the
seventeenth century, guarded by a small fort. The
Parliamentarian soldiers possessed themselves of this
in 1648, when the memorable defence of Colchester
under Lord Capel, Sir Charles Lucas, and Sir George
Lisle rendered it necessary to hold all approaches to
that town. The island at this time was said to be
very unhealthy, a statement which may have been
dictated by policy, for during the Roman occupation
it was considered so salubrious that a considerable
settlement is known to have flourished there. Traces
of the conquerors of the world have been discovered
in abundance in the parish of West Mersea—the very
church is actually built on the site of an important
villa of some Roman praetor, who, to quote the
author of *Essex Excursions*, published in 1818, ' might
have been invited by the delightfullness of the situation to make this his summer abode '. It is a fact
that during the eighteenth century an immense
amount of tessellated pavements were found beneath
the surface of the land adjacent to the church, and
of these some very precise details have been pre-

EAST BAY, COLCHESTER

Fred Roe

served. The churchyard is said to be literally based upon pavements of multiform designs, which actually extend under the chancel of the church, while the west tower, which dates from the pre-Conquest years of the eleventh century, is quoined with Roman bricks, reaved from the ruins of the destroyed buildings. The proximity of the celebrated oyster-beds

'Bygones' from old-time smugglers' haunts, Stour Valley
1. Owler's lantern used on the Essex marshes
2. Seventeenth-century wine bottle from the Stour
3. Rummer inscribed 'E. Warner, Harwich'
4. Seventeenth-century wrought iron fire dog, one of a pair

might probably be some inducement in settling the patrician's choice for his site of a residence. For wherever we find traces of Roman occupation there are oyster-shells also. Judging from the scantiness of other evidences in this country one might well be led to suppose that the principal occupations of the Romans were making pavements and eating oysters.

A couple of hundred yards east of the church still remain the foundations of a remarkable building, unearthed by chance in 1896. It is round in shape, with six spokes radiating from the centre, and twelve projections beyond the outer wall, the materials employed being Roman brick and rubble. Learned authorities have theorized that this once formed the base of a Pharos or lighthouse, but much controversy has raged over the matter, which has never been settled satisfactorily.

On the west side of Mersea Island up Virley Creek lies the hamlet from which that inlet takes its name. And here again we may well quote Baring-Gould, whose description could not be bettered.

' Salcot is a small village of old cottages at the head of a creek that opens out of the Blackwater. It has a church with a handsome tower built of flints, but no chancel ' (a chancel has been built since this was written). ' Within a bowshot, across the creek, connected with it by a bridge, is Virley Church, a small hunch-backed edifice in the last stages of dilapidation, in a graveyard unhedged, unwalled ; the church is scrambled over by ivy, with lattice windows bulged in by the violence of the gales and a bellcot hanging on one side like a drunkard. Near this decaying church is a gabled farm, and this and a cottage form Virley Village. The principal population congregates at Salcot, across the wooden bridge, and consisted—a hundred years ago—of labourers, and men more or less engaged in the contraband trade. Every house had its shed and stable, where was a donkey and cart, to be let on occasions to carry smuggled goods inland. At the end of the village stands a low tavern, the " Rising Sun ", a mass of gables ; part of it, the tavern-drinking room, is only one storey high, but the rest is a jumble of roofs and lean-to buildings, chimneys and ovens, a miracle of picturesqueness.'

Four years after these lines were published (1880) a severe earthquake jarred this part of Essex. Thirty churches and other places of public worship were rendered more or less shaky, and considerably over twelve hundred houses. Much of the ruins of Virley Church went down, and Salcot was so much damaged that restoration of the church became necessary on a large scale. A local tradition used to be voiced that the churches of Salcot and Virley were built respectively by two sisters, who agreed so little in other matters that they decided each to have their own place of worship. Since the nave of Salcot (its oldest part) was built not previous to the first half of the fourteenth century, while fragments of the ruin of Virley undoubtedly belong to the early part of the thirteenth century, this legend may be as heavily discounted as those of similar character in other parts of the country.

Of the interior of Virley Church the Rev. S. Baring-Gould was even less complimentary.

'The dedication of Virley Church is unknown.' (Actually it was dedicated to St. Mary the Virgin, but to resume :—) 'No saint in the calendar could be associated with such a church and keep his character. St. Nicholas is the patron saint of fishers, St. Giles of beggars, but who among the holy ones would spread his mantle over worshippers who were smugglers or wreckers ? ' . . . 'Virley Church is not bigger than a stable that consists of two stalls and a loose box, whereof the loose box represents the

chancel. When the curate-in-charge preached from
the pulpit—the rectors of the two parishes were
always non-resident—they kept a curate between
them—he was able to cuff the boys in the West
gallery who whispered, cracked nuts, or snored.'
We read that the bellringer stood in the gallery,
where space was so constricted that his knuckles
suffered with the upcast of the rope, when ' an oath,
audible throughout the sacred building, boomed
between the clangours of the bell '.

' Virley Church possessed one respectable feature,
a massive chancel-arch, but that gaped ; and the
pillars slouched back against the wall in the attitude
of the Virley men in the village street waiting to
insult the women as they went by.

' On either side of the east window hung one table
of the Commandments, but a village humorist had
erased all the " nots " in the Decalogue ; and it
cannot be denied that the parishioners conscientiously
did their utmost to fulfil the letter of the law thus
altered.' . . . ' The altar was a deal table, much
wormeaten, with a box beneath it. The altar possessed no cover save the red cotton pocket-handker-
chief of the curate cast occasionally across it. This
box contained the battered Communion plate, an
iron-moulded surplice with high collar, a register-
book, the pages glued together with damp, and the
brush and pan.

' The Communion rails had rotted at the bottom ;
and when there was a Communion the clerk had to
caution the kneelers not to lean against the balustrade,
lest they should be precipitated upon the sanctuary
floor.

' No such controversy as that which has of late

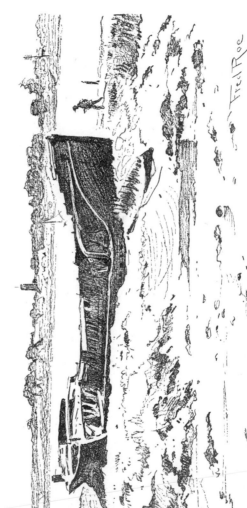

Old Wreck on The Naze

LAST MOORINGS : AN OLD WRECK ON THE NAZE

Fred Roe

3

years agitated the Church of England relative to the position of the celebrant could have affected Virley, for the floor in the midst, before the altar, had been eaten through by rats, emerging from an old grave, and exposed below gnawed and mouldy bones beneath the boards.' Truly a most instructive pen-picture of a country church in Georgian days.

Baring-Gould gives a lively, though all too brief, glimpse of Wivenhoe during regatta time. The description of Mr. Charles Pettican's residence, with 'Medusa's' figurehead and the mast on the lawn, is excellent: the wooden house with its emerald green shutters and gilded balcony, and the tiled roof which 'looked very red, as though red ochred every morning by the housemaid after she had pipeclayed the walls'. Various houses have been suggested as the original of the old shipbuilder's residence, but the author of *Mehalah* probably only described a type of abode which is very usual in such river-side settlements as Wivenhoe.

CHAPTER IV

'FOREIGNERS'

THE subject of foreigners touches me shrewdly when I penetrate into ultra-sylvan Essex, for I, with scarce a drop of any but English blood in my veins and half Essex by descent, have often been accounted a foreigner. I do not live in Essex, and have never resided in that county, but to many of the old-fashioned country folk there any-one is a foreigner if he only ventures even a few miles distant from his own locality. A good part of the excessively hot summer of 1911 I spent at Maldon and Heybridge, and learned my first lesson on the subject of 'foreigners' there. It was a summer of Italian skies, drought, and parched fields, and the sunsets across the Essex lowlands were so brilliant and multicoloured that they were marvellous to behold. Within the lock at Heybridge Basin a Scandinavian timber barque had been unlading all day, and the crew, I understand, had gone off to fill themselves up with liquor at Maldon. Yet against the walls of the 'Ship' Inn, at the lock gates, were some forms, and here was congregated the usual knot of gossipers from the adjoining cottages. The sunset was deepening into a succession of ravishing colours as a tall man strode up the incline and stopped in front of the merry-makers. I can see the man now, a well-built fellow of the labouring class, fustian clad, and with a ragged tawny moustache descending in Viking fashion over his lower jaw. His boots were white with dust from the roads, and slung over his shoulder was a rush satchel. A typical East Anglian, with not a bad face, and a tired manner.

Conversation instantly ceased, and the Heybridge group looked blankly at the new arrival.

' Evenin', mates,' he ventured.

' Evenin',' came the very distant response.

' Warmer than ever,' continued the new-comer.

' That's so.'

' I be going up to Stubbing's,' volunteered the tall man.

' Ay.'

The man did not sit down, but leaned on the stout stick he was carrying as though fatigued. Obviously he was not wanted. The sunset was on his face and I noticed that his eyes were bright blue. There was a curiously pensive look about him, as if wishful for companionship. In another class of life he would have been a dreamer.

Not another word would the cronies vouchsafe but impenetrable monosyllables. The tall man finished his modest half-measure of ale, and bidding the others good night strode off towards Maldon through the light mist which was already rising from the canal.

' They seemed to treat that man pretty coolly,' I remarked to an onlooker.

' Like as not,' was the reply; ' whoy, he's a foreigner.'

' A foreigner,' I queried; ' he looked British enough.'

' That may be, but he's a foreigner.'

' He seemed a decent sort of fellow.'

' Very like, but a foreigner. And we don't hold with suchlike. He comes from Goldhanger.'

Goldhanger being some four or five miles away.

The unwelcome intruder having departed conversation and laughter recommenced.

' I suppose if that Goldhanger man is a foreigner,' I remarked, ' I, who live so much farther away, am also one.'

' Course you be,' decidedly. ' You're a foreigner right enough.'

This little episode served to explain many things which I subsequently noticed.

*   *   *   *   *

A very few years ago, when the Eastern Counties were trying to get into regular swing again after the termination of the Great War, I took a brief spell of rest at Mountnessing, remarkable for nothing that I know of but its church, its windmill, and its association with *Lady Audley's Secret*. There was a picturesque old hand who pottered about the inn doing odd jobs, and after receiving several small tips for allowing me to sketch his rugged face ' Owd Charley ' opened himself up to me. ' Yes, you're a foreigner here, sure, but you're no' a bad 'un,' he sagely observed.

He told me his age with great pride, adding with emphasis, ' I've been a traveller in my time.'

' That is interesting,' I remarked ; ' the folks round here don't seem to travel about much.'

' No, not they,' replied ' Owd Charley '. ' Why, Mrs. —— is getting on for eighty an' she's never been to Brentwood. No, nor even to Ingatestone either. But I've been a traveller, I have.'

' Have you ever crossed over to France ? '

' France ! No,'—the old man spat contemptu-

Fred Roe

OLD POST MILL, MOUNTNESSING

ously into a ditch,—' but I've been as far as Suffolk,
I have. Twice I've been to Suffolk.'

I pondered on the vastness of such an enterprise.
The nearest point of Suffolk is close on thirty miles
distant. ' Owd Charley ' mistook my silence for
admiration and became communicative. ' Happen
you've heard of the burglary last night ? ' he inquired.

' At the Farm yonder ? '

' Aye. That be the third about here in four
days.'

The subject did not interest me very much and I
dismissed it. During the afternoon I walked over
to Ingatestone, and came back in the cool of the
evening. Next morning ' Owd Charley ' informed
me that another burglary had taken place—this
time at Ingatestone. It happening to be market-
day at Brentwood, I caught an omnibus and spent
some hours there, inspecting that wonder of medieval
inn-yards at the ' White Hart '. The following morning ' Owd Charley ' mentioned that two burglaries
had taken place at Brentwood—one of them in broad
daylight. I did not perceive any application in this
remark until returning towards my inn for lunch I
came upon ' Owd Charley ' holding a horse on the
sward-edge opposite. He motioned to me mysteri-
ously, and I went across.

' They're in there,' he said significantly, and his
eyes twinkled.

' Whom do you mean ? '

' They,' he fenced with caution. ' Happen you
don't want to meet 'em.'

I could not make out what the man meant, till
going through the yard to the private entrance I
found the landlord being interrogated by two stiff-

built typical country policemen in plain clothes. There was no mistaking them : a couple of bigger buck bobbies I have never seen. All eyes were upon me instantly. I understood now, and it amused me very much. Not a word was spoken by the executives of the law, but, as I purposely emerged to make some few commonplace remarks to mine host, my person and appearance were scrutinized very thoroughly by the two plain-clothes men. And my folding easel was an item of peculiar interest to them.

During the evening the landlord casually informed me that owing to the many thefts which had occurred during the last few days he thought it advisable to let his big dog loose in the yard that night. (My sitting-room window opened out on to the inn-yard.) He appeared a trifle perplexed the next morning, for his dog had given no sign, and yet another house-breaking had occurred in the vicinity.

' Did you come across 'em, sir ? ' inquired ' Owd Charley ', with the proud assurance of one who had given a ' foreigner ' (but no' a bad 'un) a friendly tip to keep out of sight of the Brentwood officers. They were foreigners too, and what good had they ever done ' Owd Charley ' ? Some vague bewilderment was visible on his nubbly face at my indifference.

I do not know whether any more burglaries took place in the neighbourhood after my departure, but it is a fact that pertinent inquiries followed me to my home, and then, I suppose, some fresh line was taken up, for I heard no more. If the foregoing could happen in our own time, what must have been the woes of the foreigner in the Middle Ages.

*　　　*　　　*　　　*　　　*

On another occasion, I wished to inspect the fine

old church of Laindon, with its fifteenth-century
timber priest's-house and tower. For constitutional
reasons I decided to approach it from Brentwood, and
take a look at the surrounding country. I passed
the martyr's tree and was pounding along the high
road crossing Brentwood Common when I was over-
taken by a very stout farmer, driving an antiquated
dog-cart. The man looked at me inquiringly, and I
returned his stare. He presently disappeared, a

Old Thatched Cottage, Horndon-on-the-Hill

speck in the distance. Ingrave and Herongate were
passed, and subsequently that over-renovated old
inn, the 'Bell', at Horndon-on-the-Hill. Beyond this
I stopped to make a sketch of an extraordinary cottage, with a roof of unusual pitch, and then strode
for Laindon across the fields. It was rough walking,
and I arrived at Laindon tired out. At a hotel I
entered and asked for some tea. There, regarding me

curiously, was the very stout farmer who had passed me near Brentwood.

'Didn't I see you t'other gate?' he asked uncouthly.

'What do you mean by t'other gate?' I countered.

'Coming out Brentwood way.'

'Very likely,' I admitted.

'You be a foreigner,' he observed suspiciously. 'How'd you get to Laindon?'

'I walked it.'

'You walked all that way! What for?'

'Because I like walking.'

Growing distrust and unbelief were apparent on the man's face. 'That be damned for a lie,' he growled, and went out, banging the door.

On the facts recorded I must admit that any one who walks for the sake of doing so runs some risk of being regarded as a probable criminal or a congenital idiot.

ACROSS THE MUD FLATS, CANVEY

Fred Roe.

CHAPTER V

THE OLD INNS OF ESSEX—I

NOT many years ago the cry was ubiquitous, 'Alas, for our old inns, once the finest in the world. What are they coming to?' Their meagre resources and hospitality often found a parallel in that scrap of dialogue afforded by a once popular burlesque on the drama of *The Corsican Brothers*.

'Sit down, young man. Wilt have the red or the white wine?'

'Oh, thanks! I will have the red wine.'

'Um! There is no red wine.'

But a very great improvement has taken place of recent years, and old English liberality in the way of entertainment may be found in many a country-side hostel, where, late in the nineteenth century, biscuits and cheese were most likely the sole edibles to be obtained by hungry travellers. Whether the motoring boom has anything to do with this is a moot point. I have heard evidence both for and against, from those best qualified to know the truth. To my mind whether conditions are favourably or adversely affected depends a good deal on the locality. I have lunched and dined excellently in plenteous company at hostelries which were formerly silent, gloomy and poorly served; while not five miles away on the same road an anxious-looking host has contemplated a very different state of affairs. Week-ends spent along the Great Main Road of Essex exhibit an endless procession of motors—motors, continually passing, from London, eastwards, during the mornings, and in the evenings back, westwards, towards the Great Babylon again. Through some villages they flash without a stop either way, and the only horse-drawn vehicle to be seen is an early milk-cart.

At one cosy-looking establishment, with a curious sign, up a tremendously picturesque road, I, in my wanderings, entered and asked for a meal. No, they had nothing to eat in the place. If I wanted food, I had better go to the restaurant, a few yards farther on the other side of the road. To the ' restaurant ' I accordingly proceeded, only to discover a wan little tea-shop, with a few jars of sweets in the window, beside which was a shallow tray containing five indigestible-looking pastries, plentifully sprinkled with dead flies. The thing was impossible. I retraced my way to the inn, and reopened negotiations. The landlady stood me out that she had nothing to eat in the house. I gently reminded her of certain conditions attaching to her licence. Still there was no prospect.

' You have a large fowl-roost,' I persisted. ' How about eggs ? '

' Oh, of course we have eggs.'

' And a good kitchen garden. How about a salad ? '

She had not thought of that.

The baker's cart was outside at that very moment. There would be no difficulty about the staff of life. In the end I won my way against bucolic obstinacy, and made a wholesome and satisfying meal in an old panelled room, evidently intended for refectorial purposes. But I sighed when the archives of my recollection carried me back to St. Riquier, near Abbeville in France. One sunny Sunday I had found myself in that little place, and at a modest *auberge*, near the *Beffroi*, somewhat diffidently inquired about *déjeuner*. There was not a customer in the house, nor did it seem likely that any would be immediately forthcoming, but in less than a quarter of an hour madame had dished up as nice a ' big breakfast ' as any one would wish to have : vegetable soup, an omelette, cold fowl, salad, and cheese.

With almost precisely the same materials ready at hand I can only attribute the slackness of the Essex landlady to a stubborn want of initiative. Either that or the prospect of having to bestir herself a little for the benefit of a ' foreigner '. And yet such personages will often complain that their establishments do not pay.

The traditions attaching to some of our ancient hostelries are treated with varying respect in different parts of the country. In certain licensed houses their reputed connexion with celebrities is not only treated with the greatest respect—not to mention blind faith—but no opportunity is neglected of exploiting these traditions. Others care so little for historical affinities that not an effort is made by the owners to preserve any records of association with personages of note. A few of the humbler hostelries are practically kept alive by legends, more or less spurious, of relations with that arch-scoundrel, Dick Turpin. On the other hand, the demolition of so striking a relic as the ' Nelson Room ', in that fine old hostelry, the ' Three Cups ' at Harwich, ought surely

4

to have been avoided in a patriotic country.   Parts
of the building belong undoubtedly to the sixteenth
century, while portions of more modern accommodation were re-modelled in the classic style which
prevailed during the latter years of the eighteenth
century.   But the oak overmantel and panelling of the
room which the greatest of all our admirals occupied
was a production of the seventeenth century and its

Courtyard of the ' Three Cups ' Hotel, Harwich

aspect when cared for must have been both dignified
and comfortable.   Of late years the apartment, in
spite of its reputation, was neglected : its ceiling
sagged and its floors became unsafe.   And now
another remembrance of the great has gone—to make
way, it is said, for a garage.   But despite its loss the
' Three Cups ' remains a wonderful hostel.   The
bressummers in its picturesque, flagged courtyard

display the very finest of Elizabethan carvings in the way of arabesques, and the moulded and beamed ceilings in more than one part of the house bear witness to the stout thoroughness with which builders of the early sixteenth century did their work. The most ancient portions of this hotel must have been in existence something like 150 or 160 years, when the great naval scrap between the Dutch fleet and the English came off in 1666. The combat, which was hotly contested, lasted all day till seven in the evening, and its varying fortunes were watched by a crowd of spectators which collected on Beacon Hill, close to Harwich. We can imagine the rejoicings attending our victory which were carried on at the ' Three Cups ' during this and subsequent evenings. The structure of the present tap-room must certainly have witnessed these scenes.

In the case of that fine old hostelry the ' King's Head ', at Chigwell, no pains are spared to preserve both its Dickensian traditions and its ancient features. In recent years some necessary additions have been made, but they are in tasteful harmony with the original building, which has not been interfered with in any way. For every scrap of its memorable antiquity is retained with care.

My first acquaintance with the ' Maypole ' Inn was made more years ago than I like to remember. There was no railway station anywhere near the place then, and I, a lanky youth, had to make my approach from Woodford through beautiful forest roads, less sprinkled with houses than at the present time. Afternoon was closing in when the gabled bulk of the building loomed up on the summit of a distant rise. It was quiet enough in those days, except when a cyclists'

club made the ancient house their sing-song quarters
pro tem. This happened to be one of their festive
nights. The 'Chester Room' was filled to over-
flowing, and after supper I was perforce an unwilling
witness to such recitations as 'The Charge of the
Light Brigade' and 'The Pauper's Christmas', sandwiched between choruses of rousing lustiness. The
village street was deserted, and the churchyard opposite very dark when the bugle blew, and the troop
departed, a long string of bicycle lanterns flickering
downhill like will-o'-the-wisps into the night. And
then I retired to rest, though not in the 'Maypole's'
plume-capped bed as depicted by George Cattermole.

Next day the landlord, a fine old-fashioned specimen of his class, allowed me every facility to make a
finished study of the elaborate carved fireplace in the
'Chester Room'. I well recall a narrative which he
regaled me with, and will repeat it, as nearly as
possible, in his own words.

'A good many years ago, before I became licensee,
I was told by my predecessor that one day two gentlemen came in and ordered a meal. They had a table
in this room, by the window, close to where you are
sitting. At the finish they called the landlord up,
and asked if he could let them have a bottle of good
port to end up with. He said, " Yes, gentlemen, I
can," and went down to the cellar and brought up a
bottle of 18——. He served them with this and they
tasted it. One of them said politely, " Will you take
a glass of wine with us, landlord ? "

' " Thank you, sir, I will. Here's my best
respects."

' They had a bit of a chat about the old house,
and my predecessor could see that it was not the first

time the gentleman had been here. Landlord drank his wine up, and was just going to leave the room when the gentleman who'd been talking to him said, "I suppose, landlord, you don't happen to know me."

'"No, sir," he said; "I haven't that pleasure."

'"My name is Charles Dickens," says the gentleman.

The King's Head Chigwell.

Fred Roe

The original of the 'Maypole Inn', in 'Barnaby Rudge'

'"And mine," says the other, rather pompously, "is John Forster."'

This recital took place, as I said, many years ago, but I well remember old B—— as he told the tale, his spare, erect figure, clad in tail coat with flapped pockets, and sporting gaiters, his fresh-coloured face flanked with a fringe of white whiskers. I have no doubt whatever about the accuracy of his account.

The farewell look that I took on the occasion of my first departure from the ' King's Head ' was at the picturesque room where ' the guest himself, seeing small comfort in the yet unkindled wood opened a lattice in the distant window and basked in the sickly gleam of cold March sun '.

Dickens's description of the apartment which takes its name from the precise aristocrat who was escorted to it in Chapter X of *Barnaby Rudge,* was fancifully embroidered, in common with his account of the rest of the house, yet the ' Chester Room ' certainly answers to it in many respects. But nothing like Cattermole's fireplaces and quasi-Tudor buildings have ever existed. Clever as the drawings are, the wonder is that Dickens ever passed them to illustrate *Barnaby Rudge* without a protest. Cattermole's totally imaginary picture of the ' Maypole's best room ' represents the fireplace as being an immense stone structure, with an arcade of Gothic niches filled with statuettes along its front. The fireplace which actually exists is, with its overmantel, a pedimented and pilastered elevation of wood, dating from Carolean times, the panelling of the room being somewhat later. The sole respect in which Cattermole's presentment agrees with facts is that both overmantels, the real and the imaginary, reach to the ceiling. Nor does Fred Barnard's illustration of the meeting between Chester and Haredale present any greater truth about the fireplace. The only saving grace is that you do not see so much of it. A great deal of argument has been expended on the subject of the incongruities of Dickens's illustrators, but it is extremely doubtful if any one will ever produce anything more comfortably in unison with the brilliant word-pictures in his text than Hablot K. Browne, George Cattermole and Fred Barnard. An edition of the works of Charles Dickens illustrated with unde-viating regard to fidelity—if such a thing were possible —would be in the nature of a dreadful anomaly.

I have more than once been gravely informed that the ' King's Head ' could not have existed at a time prior to the Restoration, its name (in memory of the Martyred Monarch) being against such a possibility. It has, however, never been proved that the present ancient premises were always used in the capacity of a licensed house. On the contrary, there seems to be good evidence that early in the nineteenth century the building was occupied as a boarding-school, the then ' King's Head ' being situate in some adjacent tenements. Also, for centuries prior to this the Forest Courts were held at Chigwell, and it has been suggested with a show of reason that the picturesque gabled edifice now known as the ' King's Head ' may have been primarily erected for the purpose of housing these courts.

Anyhow the hospitality of the ' King's Head ' is good these days. Long may its sign sway in the Essex breeze !

CHAPTER VI

THE OLD INNS OF ESSEX—II

COLCHESTER is full of old inns, many of them of great antiquity. The 'Red Lion', one of the finest of ancient hotels in the whole country, must have been established as a house of public entertainment some hundred and fifty years prior to those troubled days when Fairfax's cannon battered the walls of the castle, in which a band of desperate Cavaliers held out for the King. The 'Red Lion' is probably the oldest building which still sports the sign of a licensed house in Colchester. Parts of it actually date from *circa* 1400, but there are other medieval hostelries—or portions of them at least—which run it pretty close for antiquity. And under properly applied modern methods, great age certainly does not militate against comfort. It is a matter for wonder that the Parliamentarian artillery fire, which partly ruined the tower of St. Martin's Church, and brought down so much of the ancient Priory of St. Botolph, should have spared so many domestic buildings in the town. Again and again, when houses fronted with respectable Georgian brick have been demolished to make way for some unsightly up-to-date business premises, evidences have been brought to light of timber structures with cusped window mullions, and king-posts in their roofs. Fragments of these continue to be stored in the castle for all to

56

FIFTEENTH-CENTURY HOUSE, WEST STOCKWELLSTREET, COLCHESTER, BEFORE RESTORATION

Fred Roe.

see. Astonishment can only be felt at the sheer bad taste of our Georgian and Victorian forefathers which prompted them to cover up and conceal evidences of earlier art, and reduce the *façades* of buildings and apartments to a level of dull flatness. Until the summer of 1914, the front of the ' Red Lion ' retained only one small portion of the Gothic tracery, on its front, visible to the eye ; the rest had been plastered up and effaced as being contrary to respectable public taste. In the year mentioned, the whole front of the building underwent a drastic process of unpicking, with the result that an almost uninterrupted series of panels of fifteenth-century design (slightly flamboyant in character) was exposed to view. The *façade* of the ' Red Lion ', as now visible, presents one of the most remarkable sights in the Eastern Counties. It is quite as wonderful as that marvel of timber construction, the street front of Staple Inn in Holborn (saved from demolition by the Prudential Assurance Co.), and certainly antedates the London relic by many generations.

' In my 'pinion,' remarked a pig-faced countryman, within my hearing, ' they owd things all want pullin' down, an' good brick housen builded in their place.'

Well, such a course has been tried many a time before, but the old craftsmen did their jobs soundly, and it has often been discovered, when too late, that to destroy their work is neither an easy nor a paying task. Not so with the jerry-built structures, run up on their sites, which soon grow shaky and become a source of endless expense. In the meantime yet another precious heritage of our past has been lost.

The ' George ', on the opposite side of the way to

the ' Red Lion ', is apparently just one of those comfortable flat-fronted coaching hotels which may be
met with in so many of our country towns.   But
incorporated in the building are the remains of an
early fifteenth-century hall, which can only be detected
by the peculiar construction of beams and trusses,
finished by a king-post with embattled capital, which,
oddly enough, now forms the principal feature at the
head of a Georgian staircase leading to the bedrooms.
The gatehouse, through which entrance to the courtyard of the ' George ' is made from the lane, is a fine
piece of sixteenth-century timber-work.

.   The ' Marquis of Granby ', on North Hill, is
another of Colchester's ancient hostels which was
successfully unpicked about the same time as the
' Red Lion '.   This building, which dates from the
early part of Henry VIII's reign, has, however, never
been an establishment of anything like the magnitude
of that in the High Street.   The ' Marquis of Granby '
has been restored quite sufficiently, but some very
interesting features are to be found incorporated in
the modern work.   There is some beautiful linen
panelling remaining in the door of a cupboard, and
the wall-posts which support the richly decorated
beam in the ceiling of the main room are surmounted
with figures habited in costume of the early part of
the sixteenth century.   This house exhibits no ecclesiastical emblems in its decorative carving, but it
must have been some quarter of a century old when
the Reformation swept the land, and John Beche,
the last Abbot of St. John's, was hanged in front of
his own Abbey gate in 1539.

The old inns of Essex are numberless, and a great
proportion of them, for evidences of antiquity, would

SEVENTEENTH-CENTURY OUTER STAIRCASE,
THE SUN INN, DEDHAM

bear comparison with those in any other county in England. To antiquaries the ' Woolpack ' at Coggeshall, with its trussed roof of fifteenth-century date ; the ' Sun ' Inn at Feering, with its magnificent chimney-beam and pilastered porch ; the ' White Hart ', with its comfortable parlour, and the five-gabled ' Spread Eagle ', both at Witham ; the ' Sun ' at Dedham, with its rare exterior staircase ; the ' Marlborough Head ', with its superb carved ceiling in the same little town ; and the ' White Hart ', at Man-

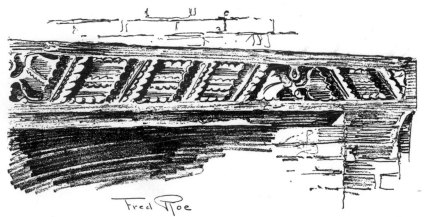

Detail of Fireplace in the ' Sun Inn ', Feering

ningtree, are all worth more than casual inspection.

In September 1804, at the height of the coaching age, ' A very young Lady,' Miss Susan Nichols to wit, made the then strenuous journey from Canonbury to Aldborough and back by Harwich, Colchester, etc. This youthful personage has left a journal of the excursion, which describes inns and towns on the route with great *naïveté*, though her rhyming and scansion are not all that can be described. Of the

'Blue Posts' at Witham—a hostelry no longer in existence—she writes :

> 'The rooms are so clean, so delicious the diet,
> The landlord so civil, so spruce and so quiet,
> The servants all round so desirous to please,
> That you find yourself here most completely at ease.'

This description, however immature, gives a good picture of the comforts of an Essex inn on the main road some century and a quarter ago.

In the 'White Hart' at Brentwood we have a remarkable survival of the fifteenth-century galleried inn. Unlike so many of its brethren, this house has not changed its conditions through force of circumstances. It was undoubtedly built and originally intended for its present purpose, and seemingly no lapse in this continuity has ever occurred during all the centuries since it first came into existence. The earliest part of the structure is the gallery round the yard, with its open range of arches. This may date from the first half of the fifteenth-century, and the very name of the hostel is most likely a reminiscence of yet an older structure which sported as its sign the badge of Richard II. But very few of our ancient inns retain any history to speak of, and all that is known with any certainty of the 'White Hart' at Brentwood is that it was actually an inn under that sign in Elizabeth's reign, and was a well-known house of call for coaches during the eighteenth and early nineteenth centuries.

If we are surprised at the paucity of information as to the annals of our old inns, what could be said on the subject of their ancient furniture ? In how many of them are any relics of their household goods retained ? We can all of us recollect, without the

THE 'LOBSTER SMACK' INN, CANVEY ISLAND

Fred Roe

slightest effort, a plurality of ' Red Lions ', ' Suns ',
' White Harts ', ' Angels ', and ' Georges ', exhibiting
traces of bygone splendour, whose appointments are
now of the gross mahogany and stuffed-horsehair
order, usual replacements of the Elizabethan and
Jacobean styles, and relics of a period when transit
by horsed vehicle was about to be superseded by the
railway.   Only too often such innovations are sadder
still, and the varnish and plush of Tottenham Court
Road remains very much in evidence in this insane
endeavour to bring the establishments ' up to date '.

As a set off against these offences may be accounted
the sturdy independence of the proprietors of a few
places of entertainment, whose ownership of household goods no monetary offer will tempt or shake.
It may be that the ancient furniture acts as a ' draw '
to the house, especially when any historical legends
connect them ; but this is a mere detail.

Another class may be briefly hinted at.   There is
the landlord with an eye to business, who provides
antiques for his guests, and with dangerous adapt-
ability, born of a little knowledge, does not disdain
to simulate certain desirable styles upon substructures
of plain but positive specimens.   I should like to say
quite a lot on this subject, but there is such a thing as
a law of libel in the land.

It sometimes happens that the insignia of ancient
houses of entertainment are transplanted and may be
found as waifs in localities for which they were never
intended.   To give an instance : the large carved
black effigy of an Indian, standing outside the Railway Hotel at Witham, is said to have been brought
to its present position by the former proprietor of a
house of entertainment in Shoreditch.   Whether this

is true or not, it is extremely likely that the figure was originally located at the celebrated ' Black Boy ' Hotel at Chelmsford, which house, after many vicissitudes, was finally closed down and demolished in 1857. The Eastern Counties Railway, whose terminus was formerly at Shoreditch, was responsible for many ancient inns going out of business. Other relics of the ' Black Boy ', including a fine boss carved with the combined badges of the De Veres, may also be seen in Chelmsford Museum ; and I cannot help deploring the fact that the antiquities in this museum are pretty nearly all the County Town has left to it, owing to the ' whiffling activity ' of ' improvement ' which the Municipal Authorities have shown in their disregard for any remnants of the olden times.

The ' Crossed Keys ' Inn, a fifteenth-century building of low elevation but immensely strong construction, was still standing in Moulsham Street in 1915. It was the last of Chelmsford's medieval hostelries, and was a really good specimen of ancient domestic architecture, but the roof was falling in through neglect, and it was evident that only war's exigencies delayed its destruction, to make way for a picture theatre. During the aesthetic craze of the 'eighties, the plaster between its beams had been decorated with hideous patterns of sunflowers, but the building was not past restoration and might well have been spared. The ' Crossed Keys ' has now totally disappeared, and a picture theatre, quite in keeping with the rest of Chelmsford's uninspired cheerlessness, has arisen in its place.

Maldon All Saints retains, close to its parish church, portions of a very ancient hostelry behind the uncomprisingly flat brick front of the ' Blue Boar ' Hotel.

THE LAST OF THE FRIARY, CHELMSFORD

The range of timber buildings stretching down the south side of its coaching-yard dates certainly from as far back as the commencement of the fifteenth century, and may well belong to even an earlier decade. Some twenty years ago when I first visited Maldon there used to stand, under a shed down this yard, a venerable old posting vehicle of Pickwickian appearance, evidently a survival of early nineteenth-century days, and used for cross-country travelling before railways had intersected Essex. It had been a good four-wheeler in its time, the type of useful highflier that had rushed Jingle and Miss Wardle up to London on the occasion of their elopement from Dingley Dell. The then landlord did not like to destroy it, so there the ramshackle old thing stayed on year after year, never being stirred except for a stray cleaning down by the aged ostler. The proprietorship of the ' Blue Boar ' changed, and when I subsequently visited Maldon I found that the obsolete conveyance was not.

Once a somewhat dreary establishment the ' Blue Boar ' is now as comfortable a specimen of the country hotel as could be wished for.

At Danbury, one of the most beautifully situated villages in Essex, some 380 feet above the sea level, is the ' Griffin ' Inn, a picturesque, gabled structure, dating from Elizabethan times, but much pulled about in later years. Situated midway between Chelmsford and Maldon the ' Griffin ' makes a very convenient house of call and is deservedly popular. At the time of writing the process of unpicking its half-timbered front has been partially carried out, and the whole building, after many years of injudicious plastering, is now beginning to assume something of its ancient aspect. It lies immediately facing the pathway to the church, on the breezy summit of the hill; close by is an old smithy, and on the opposite side of the road a range of early sixteenth-century tenements. A pleasant dining-room of large size with a beamed ceiling occupies the ground floor of the west wing of the inn, and from this a doorway opens out on to an old-world garden. In the quaint entrance bar some fragments of Perpendicular carving, waifs from the church screen, have been fitted. The church itself, with its venerable monuments to the St. Cleres, and the memorials to the Mildmay family, belong descriptively to another chapter. As is the case with so many of our ancient hostelries, very little is actually known of the history of the ' Griffin ' Inn, but for generations past it has aroused interest. At the commencement of the nineteenth century Joseph Strutt, the antiquary, wrote a regular Wardour Street romance entitled *Queenhoo Hall*, a work now forgotten save for one little circumstance that resulted in enormous consequences. Many of the scenes in this novel were laid at the ' Griffin ' Inn at Danbury, a locality which seemed to have a fascination for Mr. Strutt. *Queenhoo Hall* was a very long-winded production, but its author died in 1802, leaving the romance unfinished. More high-falutin nonsense in literature it would be difficult to find, and such indeed was the opinion of a rising young man who was asked by the publishers to complete the work for them. *Queenhoo Hall* was produced in 1808, with Scott's two chapters in conclusion. Some few years previous to this Scott had written a good part of *Waverley*, but thought so little of it that he put the manuscript away in a drawer, where it lay forgotten.

THE CREST OF THE HILL, DANBURY

A couple of years after *Queenhoo Hall* was published Scott by chance came across the draft manuscript of *Waverley*, and, inspired by the success of Strutt's work, felt inclined to complete his own, instead of patching up the dull effusions of other writers. How he was at first discouraged, but eventually succeeded, need not be related here ; it is sufficient to emphasize the part which that dull book incorporating the ' Griffin ' Inn played in Scott's career. *Waverley* itself was not brought out till 1814 ; the moral of the foregoing being that it took a long time to publish books in those days. *Waverley* was written for all time, but as regards *Queenhoo Hall* readers who wish to enjoy descriptions abounding in the true local colour of Essex would do well not to resuscitate it. This digression may appear somewhat superfluous ; we shall, however, meet with Mr. Strutt again in another chapter.

A fine summer day at Danbury, with the blazing sun in the open, the cool porch of the church inviting rest within, and the ' Griffin ' Inn to lunch at, is an experience not easily forgotten.

The ' Bell ', at Woodham Walter, and the ' White Hart ', at Pleshey, are both survivals of fine old Tudor hostelries, with many quaint features in the shape of half-timber framing and carved barge-boards. Older than either of these, the ' White Hart ', at Manningtree, exhibits at first sight fewer obvious evidences of great age, but there can be no doubt about the antiquity of portions of the house which remain incorporated behind the red-brick front facing the street. The moulded beams under the gateway and in the bar are superb, and must have been quite old stock at the time of our first Stuart king. They

certainly date from not later than the opening of the
sixteenth century, and may be even older. On one
of the wall-posts supporting the principal beam in
the bar is carved a human head, surrounded by a
species of frill, over which hangs a veil reminiscent of
the linen-fold pattern. A corresponding head, better
executed and in a much finer state of preservation,
exists, but is now enclosed in a dark cupboard and
difficult to see.

A few pieces of old oak furniture were still in use
at the ' White Hart ' at Manningtree when I visited it,
some of them being true and desirable. One specimen, a small dressing-table, was said to have been
presented to one of the landlord's forbears by the
great Shakespeare himself. A connoisseur of such
articles would have placed this relic somewhere during
the last twenty years of the seventeenth century.
But that is a mere detail.

Inscribed. EWW 1590

THE SWAN INN, BRAINTREE

CHAPTER VII

MORE CONTRABAND

ALL along the coast-line of Essex numerous aged inns exist, whose connexion with the smuggling traffic in bygone times can hardly be doubted. The 'Bull', at Corringham, situated on the marsh lands which border Thames Haven, is one of these. The 'Bull' is a very, very old house, for though the main part of its structure dates only from the seventeenth century, one gabled portion goes back a couple of hundred years earlier. A picturesque mixture of styles, the 'Bull' Inn stands facing the church, whose early Norman tower is one of the architectural wonders of Essex. In olden times Corringham was a very desolate spot. Although the immediate vicinity of the village is fairly well wooded nowadays, the adjacent flats skirting the sweeping intricacies of Stanford Creek are forbidding in aspect, their ramifications being a very Tom Tiddler's Ground for contrabandists and inversely a very difficult locality for combined action on the part of the revenue officers. Inter-communication with Corringham must have been exceedingly difficult in bygone centuries, for the place was so isolated that it is inconceivable that anyone would have wished to settle there by choice, unless as an anchorite. As late as only ninety years ago but one road touched the place, and that must have been in a very ill-defined condition. Nevertheless, the church, with its fourteenth-century body and its Early Norman tower, gives mute evidence that the population around must at one time have been respectable in point of numbers. One cannot but think that, hemmed in by marsh lands as it still is, and with Stanford Creek so conveniently available, the settlement was used largely as a secret ' bumping ground ' for contraband goods from very early times. The district was formerly a prolific breeding-ground for the fen ague, and when the night fog hung thick and the ' hobbie lanterns ' moved over the marsh little did it matter whether French brandy or Dutch gin had paid duty so long as it was potent—and not very expensive.

With Manningtree, nearly forty miles distant to the north-east, circumstances were decidedly different. Manningtree was situated on a recognized trade waterway, doing much business in the coasting line, and would no doubt be closely watched by the gaugers. But even here smuggling was rife. The King's Men could not be in force in half a dozen places at once, and it may be taken as a fact that certainly three-fourths of the coast-side population were more or less in sympathy with the other party. The very streets and lanes of the little town on the Stour seem to have been planned with an eye to the contraband trade. Cocklofts are said to have run through one house to another in succession, to facilitate escape from the revenue men, and sections of these overhead passages still remain in the more ancient buildings. Illicit running must have been a lucrative game in this neighbourhood during the bad old days. ' Moonshine liquor ' came here in plenty. Though why it was termed ' moonshine liquor ' I could never make

THE BULL INN, CORRINGHAM

6

out, as the stuff was necessarily run over when there was little or no chance of a moon. Gone now are the warring methods of less even than a century ago, but indications of the fascination attending the pursuit may occasionally be detected in the furtive eyes of the longshore man.

The landlord of the ' White Hart ', a fine type of the English country innkeeper, with a Georgian head, stated to me that a subterranean passage (now bricked up) existed from the cellars of that establishment down to the water-side, though how communication was kept open in the salt marsh was not explained. We must not, however, forget that there are still living people of extreme old age who declare that they have used such tunnels for the purpose indicated.

One might do worse than find oneself in the quiet main street of Manningtree on a sunny day. Various friends had previously informed me that there was nothing interesting to see there, but I found plenty. True it is that modern banking premises and other business establishments have obliterated a good deal of the old town, yet much remains. And what is left looks as though its dead past could be more than usually interesting to recount. In one tall house, in South Street, with a particularly elevated roof, a good look-out must have been kept on the estuary for eventualities.

Dotted at remote distances along the foreshore of the Stour are various odd-looking timber-built huts, many of them of great age, and used nowadays for storing ships' gear in. The dual purposes they were once put to brings to mind Arthur Morrison's description of ' Joe Furber '. 'A bit of a smuggler himself, though a boat-builder in the main.' So many of the water-side characters did a little gambling in this side line that nothing particular was thought of it.

In the bar-parlours of numerous old inns in such towns as Harwich the skippers congregate and spin their yarns. The tobacco they smoke may or may not be smuggled, but, according to W. W. Jacobs, ' It is well known all along the water-side that this greatly improves the flavour.' These old shell-backs are well worth listening to : however prolix they wax, their conversation rarely becomes anaesthetic. Rum, their favourite tipple, is in demand, yet as one of them sagely remarked, he hadn't had more than would baptize a fairy. I heard one weather-beaten veteran call to the attendant damsel for ' a drop of Nelson's blood, miss ', and the order was understood and promptly executed.

In the open streets and lanes of Harwich many features exist, which to the discerning eye bear obvious evidences of the former prosperity of the place as a maritime port ; but more remain hidden in cupboards and back yards remote from the public gaze. More still exist of the old-time smuggling trade, though inaccessible to the curious. Unseen by the wayfarer, Harwich is literally honeycombed with subterranean passages and caverns, a labyrinth once used to great effect by evaders of the revenue, but now choked up and forgotten. There is no romance in this case. Residents in the old town are occasionally reminded of the existence of these mysterious dens when efforts are made to bring the streets more up to date. Some ancient house is condemned and pulled down, leaving an unsightly gap in the jumbled

HIGH-PITCHED ROOF, MANNINGTREE

mass of habitations. Over and over again such demolition reveals gloomy passages under the foundations branching away into obscurity, some of them wide enough to drive a horse and cart through. Pillars are even said to support the vaulting in places. Quite useless in these days, the cavities are mostly filled up with rubbish, shot from the destroyed premises as the readiest way of getting rid of it, and so silent evidences of smuggling days and smuggling

Hut on the Marshes, Manningtree

ways once more disappear. No testimony remains as to when these passages were first excavated, though presumably they were the growth of ages. Most of them are too large for water-courses or drains, although they may incidentally have been used as such.

In 1845 was first published a novel by G. P. R. James, entitled *The Smuggler*, a tiresome tale that nevertheless displays an intimate knowledge of the

equivocal relations that existed between the contrabandists and a great many of the magistrates.
James's novels—a tremendous array—are little read
nowadays, but their author could look back to a
period in his own life when smuggling was at its
height. In Chapter XIII of *The Smuggler* the parti-
ality which was shown by the Bench to the son of one
of the justices, and his expedient acquittal, are well
told, and atone for much that is undoubtedly very
commonplace in the book. We know that parts of
this work were founded on actual records concerning
the famous Rainsley gang, and this incident may be
one of them. The locality chosen is in the vicinity
of Hythe, in Kent, and not in Essex, but the principle
involved was on very similar lines all along the coast.
Harwich at one time contained a great many mansions or houses of good class, and it is hardly con-
ceivable that subterranean passages could have been
excavated to any extent without some connivance
on the part of those in authority. Indeed, some
doubtful proceedings appear to have been carried
out almost openly under the very noses of the guard-
ians of the revenue. No contemporary records of
this complacency, whenever it existed, on the part
of the old magistracy towards smuggling, can be
found in cold print. It is not likely that any official
account would be entered in the legal minutes of such
times, while with the more humble part of the population the covert aside, ' Leave us a keg ', would
generally be responded to in a manner sufficient to
silence all evidence. In 1826 Turner's *Views on the
Southern Coast of England* was first published, and
in the exquisite plate of Folkestone we see a party
of men, in striped caps, busily engaged in digging

Fred Roe.

AN OLD-TIME SMUGGLER

a ' hide ' for some tubs which they have hauled up
to the top of the cliff. All this in broad daylight too !
We must make some allowance for the exuberance of
the great artist's imagination. If tubs were buried
at all in such a perceptible spot, it would certainly
not be in bright sunshine, and yet the incident may
have been meant to typify the attitude of toleration
which was displayed to the traffic in certain localities.

Doorhead (1588), *Harwich*

In the sixteenth century Harwich was evidently
in a very prosperous state, for many palatial residences existed there, notably in the junction of
Market Street with King's Head Street, where evidences of them still linger. It was however at a
house, said to be ' in the central part of High Street ',
that Queen Elizabeth resided during her visit to the
town in 1561. So prosperous was Harwich then that
the corporation politely declined to ask any favours

of Her Majesty on her departure, which drew from
the Virgin Queen the remark, ' A pretty town and
wants nothing,' which pithy observation may be
interpreted in more ways than one.

The following reign (that of James I) saw the
building of Landguard Fort, on the opposite bank of
the estuary, but the subsequent proximity of the
military element did not deter the contrabandists
from carrying on their occupation.   Relations between
the civil authorities and the military were ill defined,
and apt to become a matter for friction.   During the
eighteenth century and the early part of the nineteenth, H.M. revenue cutters were more feared by
moonlight men than whole battalions of soldiers.
This primitive type of smuggler, with his crude
methods, may be said to have come to an end at the
close of the Crimean War, for after peace had been
established the coast-guard service was reorganized
and placed upon a more effective footing, under
Naval administration.   And yet there linger a few
members of the old brigade—links with a past when
the unlawful traffic was carried out on obsolete lines.
At the time these records are being penned there is
still living at Rayleigh a nonagenarian who retains
vivid recollections of his youthful occupation in the
contraband trade and also freely admits that his
father was an inveterate smuggler before him.   The
exploits of the gang to which they belonged were
principally carried out up the Crouch, their homes
being at the Stambridges, two small villages conveniently situated between that river and the Roach.
The most startling feat of the elder M—— was to
meet habitually a landing of contraband goods with
an old travelling vehicle, the wheels of which, as well

as the horses' hoofs, were muffled, so that transit was
rendered almost noiseless. Many a belated villager
must have been terrified almost out of his wits at the
passing of this silent apparition bearing its dutiable
load, though to those ' in the know ' the vision of
old M——'s ' Ghost Bus ', as it came to be called, was
merely a token that another successful run had been
effected. And the latter folks discreetly held their

Rayleigh

peace. In the end most of the band were caught and
transported, but the ingenious owner of the ' Ghost
Bus ' escaped by clearing out of the country.

Highly ingenious were the devices resorted to by
the old-time contrabandists. The ' Spread Eagle '
Hotel at Witham, a gabled hostelry dating mainly
from the sixteenth century, has on its premises a
mysterious well, entry to which can only be obtained
from the roof. Tradition has it that kegs of smuggled

liquor used to be lowered down this cavity secure from observation—though it is possible it may have been intended for other purposes.

To those who are gifted with discerning eyes curious little reminders occasionally appear, that to the commonplace, unobservant passer-by would possess no significance whatever. One such happened to a brother brush, on whose word I can implicitly rely.

It was a somewhat foggy day in September when my artistic friend, attracted by the open doorway and mullioned windows of an ancient inn in a country street, entered what had obviously been at one time the residence of an opulent merchant. The passage opened out on to the remains of a courtyard, which was decorated with quaint little carved pilasters running up the walls. Beyond this was what had formerly been a wharf, now quiet and overgrown, and apparently unused. One side of the passage was formed by a partition which had been put in Georgian times, to keep away draughts from the principal living apartment, now relegated to the uses of a tap-room. The ceiling in this apartment was finely moulded with Tudor roses and fleurs-de-lys. The farther end of the room was partly screened off by huge winged settles, which, curving round, on either side, created a sort of snuggery near the fireplace. The hearth itself, surmounted by a big stone four-centred arch, had not been bricked up, though it had been fitted with a modern grate, in which smouldered the red glow of a wood fire. The fireplace was situated at the opposite end of the long room to the mullioned window, and it was very dark there, though, on a shelf above, some brass candlesticks and sauce-

Fred Roe

OLD HOUSES, EAST STREET,
COGGESHALL

pans of bright copper reflected points of burnished light. On one side of the grate was seated a bright-eyed old man, smoking quietly, with a fringe of beard round his face, like rays encircling the sun. He regarded my friend in silence. To him presently entered a younger man, who glanced furtively at the strange visitor. The presence of a third person in this sanctum was palpably awkward to the pair.

' Mornin',' they greeted each other with.

Ten minutes' silent smoking followed.

' Heard the news, Jarge ? ' at length inquired the last comer.

' Noa.'

' Jim's got rid of that there.'

' Well, I'm . . .'

Another silence of ten minutes, during which both men smoked hard, and looked at the gathering blaze. Then :

' Did yow say as Jim had got rid of that there a'ready ? '

' He have.'

Another enigmatical silence—of longer duration this time.

The last comer ultimately heaved himself on to his feet. ' Mornin', Jarge,' he said with a nod.

' Mornin',' responded the other, who then added impressively, ' but I never thought Jim would have got rid of that there.'

Both the worthies departed, glancing distrust-fully at my innocent friend, and leaving him in a pleasing state of perplexity as to whether what Jim had disposed of was a load of contraband tobacco, a cask of spirits, or a spavined mare.

7

CHAPTER VIII

ABOUT OLD ESSEX CHURCHES—I

ESSEX is not a stone region, for over almost the whole surface of the county extends the London clay, which will serve to explain why so many of the church towers, and even the edifices themselves, are built of brick. But the forest land, which primevally covered the greater part of the country-side, was in bygone days replete with fine oaks, stretching nearly up to the very walls of London. Oak trees of great size do not exist now in any considerable numbers, owing to such former exigencies as shipbuilding, and the construction of domestic dwellings. Stone being a scarce commodity in Essex will also account for the fact that not a few of the church towers and belfries are of wood raised on complicated substructures of huge beams of oak. In certain cases even the chancel arcades are constructed out of this material, while at the village of Stock the belfry of the church is made entirely of oak, with traceried windows of the fifteenth century pierced through solid baulks of timber. Then of the many recumbent effigies in churches we have ten remaining examples carved out of wood, instead of alabaster or stone, a higher number than in any other county in England. There used to be more of them, but vandalism has been at work, even perpetrated by those whose duty it

Fred. Roe.

THIRTEENTH-CENTURY OAK EFFIGY
IN DANBURY CHURCH

should have been to protect such memorials of antiquity. The late Mr. Miller Christy, the well-known antiquary, records that one of these relics formerly at Messing (said to be the effigy of Sir Robert Messing who built the church) was actually destroyed through the incredible ignorance of a quondam vicar, who converted it into logs for the grate. Language fails one when recounting so stupendous an act of foolishness.

Timber towers and belfries supported on elaborate substructures of wood are to be found at Mount-nessing, Margaretting, Bulphan, Thundersley, Nave-stock, West Hanningfield, Stock, Ramsden Belhouse, Laindon-cum-Basildon, Stondon Massey, Blackmore, Horndon-on-the-Hill, and other places.

Recumbent effigies of oak exist at Danbury, Elm-stead, Little Leigh, Little Horkesley, and Little Baddow. These comprise one priest, one civilian, two ladies, and six mailed knights. The periods of their construction range severally from the middle of the thirteenth century down to *circa* 1340, the earliest (that of a knight at Little Horkesley) antedating the celebrated brass of Sir John D'Abernon in Surrey by nearly thirty years. After the middle of the fourteenth century we have no more wooden effigies of this sort in Essex. But the custom of occasionally building oaken arcades in the chancels of parish churches continued right down to the seventeenth century. Part of the remaining structure of Man-ningtree Church consists of a couple of arches hewn out of oak, while the Church of All Saints, at Theydon Garnon, possesses an arcade of five bays, completely constructed of the same material and erected contemporaneously with the North Aisle, which is dated 1644. But it is at Shenfield that we find the finest instance of timber being used for arcading in place of stone. About the end of the fifteenth century, Shenfield Parish Church was enlarged by the addition of an aisle, and the north wall being cut away for this purpose, it was replaced by a noble arcading of six bays, hewn from giant oaks such as we no longer possess in the County of Essex. The columns are clustered and have capitals and bases, moulded in the Perpendicular style. Buckler, in his *Twenty-two Churches of Essex*, has a good deal to say about this wonderful arcade, and his despondency at the merciless way in which it was treated during the so-called 'improvements' made in 1840, will be shared by every true antiquary.

Red brick superseded timber and rubble in the building of belfries. There is no other county in England where so great a proportion of church towers exists in which red brick constitutes the sole material. The periods of their erection date severally from the latter part of the fifteenth century well into Henry VIII's reign. Good specimens, battlemented and turreted, exist at Ingatestone, Fryerning, Tolleshunt Major, Tollesbury, Billericay and many other places. Some of these possess such a remarkable family likeness to each other that, if they had been built nearer to our own time, we should have suspected them of being designed by the same firm.

*   *   *   *   *

Of pre-Norman work, Essex possesses what is in all probability one of the earliest Christian churches in the kingdom, and as such St. Peter-on-the-Wall, at Bradwell-on-Sea, must be regarded with feelings of the most profound veneration. Some time during

Fred Roe

TOLLESBURY

WOLVERHAMPTON
PUBLIC LIBRARIES.

the Roman occupation a fortress was established by
the Conquerors of the World on that hunch of land
which juts out six miles north of Asheldham, in a
position to dominate the estuary of the Blackwater.
Originally called Othona, this fortress, though not a
large one, was of immense strength, for vestiges of
its walls, fourteen feet thick, still survive. The
Roman sentries on the ramparts of Othona must have
ceased their vigils for something like two hundred
and fifty years before the Christian place of worship
was raised by Cedd, Bishop of the East Saxons, direct
across one section of the abandoned *Castrum*. That
the deserted fort was quarried for stone and tiles to
build St. Peter's Chapel there is abundant evidence.
Erected somewhere about the year 660, the body of
the fabric has lasted in this desolate spot till the
present time, somewhat mutilated it is true. It has
seen many vicissitudes. Up to about ten years ago
it was used in the degraded capacity of a barn, but
has since been happily restored to its original purpose.
And there to-day that remarkable building rises like
a stranded ark over the wind-swept flats, hardly anything being visible around but the lonely fields that
once held a Roman outpost. One hopes for their
own sakes that the legionaries who manned the walls of
Othona were not indigenous members of actual Roman
soil, but auxiliary guards drawn off from some outlying
province of the Empire where the climate would not
be too delightful. I for one should not be surprised
if, with the able help of Mr. Arthur Weigall, it would
be possible to arrive at the exact unit—whether
Gothic or Scythian guard—that garrisoned the fort.
But that does not come within the scope of the present
work. The locality of Bradwell may have been more

populous than we can imagine, but it is not too much to say that whether as Roman Othona, or the later Saxon Ythanceastre, it would never have been anything other than a cheerless one.

With Colchester, only a little over ten miles away to the northward, the case was different, for the con-

Fred Roe

Roman gladiators on the ' Colchester Vase '
in Colchester Castle

ditions of site and salubrity there were both excellent. Camulodunum was deservedly a great and populous place, and when, somewhere about the year 500, the Saxon invaders possessed themselves of the Anglo-Roman city there was plenty of material for the new-comers to adapt or work upon. The Saxon folk destroyed much, but they do not appear to have constructed to any great extent, at least in the way of buildings which were at all enduring. It is more than probable that the still abundant remains of the Roman occupation saved them a great deal of trouble in this way.

In the tower of the Parish Church of Holy Trinity, at Colchester, a notable relic exists, which, though some centuries later than Cedd's chapel, not only dates from pre-Conquest. times, but very likely from the period when the Danish line ruled. The walls are of rubble plentifully mixed with Roman brick, pierced with small round-headed windows, while in the western face is one of the most remarkable doorways in the whole of the country. This entrance has a triangular head surmounted by rough projecting courses, all constructed entirely of Roman brick, which material also forms the capping from which the doorhead springs. The amount of Roman brick used in this tower is very great, and induces a desire to know how the Saxon builders procured such a quantity of this material. The Romans endeavoured to build for all time, and it has frequently been found that any attempt to demolish their structures entails the greatest difficulties. The cement which bound both tiles and rubble together is so tenacious and solid that the stock material cannot be detached intact, little being possible save in the way of whole-sale smashing up. In most cases it would be practically useless to attempt to disintegrate the courses of tile without rendering them worthless. It therefore can only be surmised that enormous quantities of tiles must have been left unused at the time of the Roman evacuation, and that these brick-yards must have been left uncleared, remaining in a neglected state for several years until pressing requirements suggested employment of their contents. To me, at least, this seems the only feasible explanation. The great semicircular tower arch of Holy Trinity Church, constructed wholly of Roman materials, could have been built out of no reavings from a ruined building.

Scarcely less interesting than Holy Trinity Church, Colchester, the tower of Corringham Church, on the Stanford marshes, is one of those very early structures, which some authorities declare to be pre-Conquest, though others think it is not. One thing is certain : the building was planned with an eye to defensive as well as religious purposes. Its rubble walls for two stages are pierced only with very minute windows, which afford no possibility of entry. The only decoration on the exterior is a double blind arcading on the upper storeys of the tower, the highest possessing a single window on three of its sides. In every case the arches are constructed of rubble. The body of the church dates from the fourteenth century ; it is much restored, but contains some good brasses.

The Parish Church of Copford, four miles from Colchester, has its original chancel and apsidal end, dating from Norman times. Again, there is much Roman tiling included in the building materials. The groined vaulting of the apse is curiously Romanesque in style, and rendered more so by the decorative arrangement of a very remarkable series of mural paintings, which have undergone much, but, at the same time, judicious reparation. The painted signs of the Zodiac which adorn the arch of the apse are said to be unique survivals in this country. These paintings are reported to have been discovered in the year 1869, but it seems that so long ago as 1690 workmen, who were preparing the walls of the church for a regular good whitewashing, unexpectedly came upon them, and must have promptly proceeded to obliterate the decorations once more.

What about the silent history of Copford in periods when frightful deeds were perpetrated under the name of justice ? This church shares with other places of Christian worship the tradition that the flayed skin of a human being was stretched under the ancient ironwork of the north door. Hadstock and Benfleet likewise have this dreadful distinction, and in every case legend associates the shrivelled epidermis with the punishment of a ravaging Dane. Tradition is accurate—at least in one respect. The *Archaeologia* of Essex notes, in 1889, that portions of the skin were submitted to expert examination by the assistant Conservator to the Museum of the Royal College of Surgeons, and were conclusively determined in each case to be human. Furthermore, minute pieces of fair hair still adhered to the cuticle. No skin remains nowadays on any of the doors, indeed the very ironwork has disappeared from that at Copford, though traces of its flourished form still appear on the weathered woodwork. Now the battened door is evidently a relic of the twelfth century, which is getting distinctly late in history for marauding Danes. An ingenious theory has however been propounded by Mr. Percival J. S. Percival, in his book *London's Forest*, which seems to me more nearly to approach the truth than any other conjecture, and from this I venture to make an extract :—

' Regarded in the light of the ancient forest laws, the traditional act of sacrifice is possibly at fault. The nature of the offence might equally well have been a crime against the royal beasts of the forest. In those stern days, when Essex was part of the Danelagh, the stringent Danish law forbade the serf to hunt on peril of his skin. The penalty was stated in the precise terms : " He shall pay with his hide," and payment was made in the ratio of the estimated damage.'

This ' painful thing ', as Mr. Dowler termed the process of skinning, may well have been a survival of the old Danish laws at the time of its infliction. When I visited Copford, very soon after the close of the Great War, a fragment of this tortured human parchment was still to be seen framed in the vestry. Visitors to Colchester Castle can see another scrap of human skin that came from the door of Hadstock Church.

It will be remembered that Worcester Cathedral still possesses its old doors, dating from the thirteenth century, upon which fragments of skin still cling, flayed, in this case it is said, from the body of some unhappy wretch who so far forgot himself as to steal the sanctus bell.

Hadstock, just mentioned, lies on the Cambridgeshire border of the county, about three and a half miles east of Great Chesterford. It is most popularly known as owning one of the three churches in Essex whose doors were hide-bound with mementoes of the skin-flaying process once popular as a punishment with our semi-civilized forefathers. But the Parish Church, dedicated to St. Botolph, can lay claim to a far greater distinction, for it has been competently settled that in all human probability the present building incorporates much of the actual ' mynster ' that Canute raised as a memorial to the smashing victory which he gained over the Saxons under Edmund Ironside in the vicinity.   This fabric is preserved with wisdom tempered with moderation.   The north doorway with its rudely moulded arch and sculptured Romanesque capitals is one of the most remarkable pre-Conquest features remaining in East Anglia.

The historic little church of Greensted, near Ongar, is so venerable in its associations that the first sight of it is apt to cause something in the nature of a shock to those who expect to behold either a crumbling relic of the Dark Ages, or merely a well-preserved memorial of antiquity.   With the exception of the famous oak walls of the nave, constructed, at the lowest computation, nearly a thousand years ago, this early Christian place of worship has been so drastically renovated that the effect produced is painfully modern.   Down to the middle of the eighteenth century the fabric was entire, though suffering greatly from the effects of time.   Subsequent restorations have been carried too far, and the building wherein the bones of St. Edmund rested in 1013 might now be regarded in the light of a ' very pretty ' piece of work, were it not for those weather-scarred trunks which remain almost intact.   The all too zealous squaring-up of Shakespeare's birthplace, at Stratford-on-Avon, has a parallelism in the ' thorough job ' made of the modern alterations and embellishments to that log-built shanty which the early Christian Fathers pieced together so well at Greensted.   If a consensus of intelligent opinion could be taken on such a subject, a large majority would probably be in favour of the rational upkeep of this memorial on its original simple lines, the money collected for the purpose of trimming being devoted instead towards the erection of a more convenient building for Divine Service.   An illustration in *Vetusta Monumenta* shows plainly that in 1748 there existed only one dormer window on the south side of the church, this being probably added during the sixteenth century.   There are now three modern dormers and a heavy porch, all in a style of unsuitable Gothic—and the roof for neatness approaches suburbia as nearly as modern builders' material can make it.

' From the Fury of the Northmen, Good Lord deliver us,' ran a very ancient pre-Conquest prayer, and that entreaty with but slight modification might be applied against the case of the over-zealous restorer with too much money to spend.

WALTHAM ABBEY FROM THE MEADOWS

8

CHAPTER IX

ABOUT OLD ESSEX CHURCHES—II

BUT rare and excellent as they are, the antiquarian attractions of the temples previously mentioned pale before the wonders of Waltham Abbey Church. This noble fane, or such of it as yet exists—for only the ancient nave has been spared to us—is one of our choicest national treasures, and Dr. Thomas Fuller, for many years incumbent of the parish, spoke to the point when he said, ' In some sort the History of Waltham Church is the Church History of England.'

In the year 1030, a standard-bearer to King Canute, known as Tovi the Proud, seems to have appreciated the Forest of Wealdham so much that he founded a small village here, and built a church for the housing of a miraculous cross which had been discovered on an estate that he held in Somerset. Tovi was a wealthy man, but, as is frequently the case with such personages, his son and heir quickly dissipated his inheritance, with the result that the Lordship of Wealdham soon reverted to the Crown. Edward the Confessor subsequently granted this to Harold, by way of keeping property in the family. The monkish King Edward had married Harold's sister, and the Royal generosity was tempered by the saving condition that Earl Harold should build a monastery at the place and furnish it with all

necessaries, '*in memoriam mei et conjugis mei Eadithe*'.
Accordingly, in 1059, Harold commenced the erection
of a more splendid establishment, the consecration
of which, in May 1060, was honoured by the presence
of the Confessor himself.   This, however, could have
only been a nucleus of the grand building, which was
not completed for many years.   Six or seven years
after the consecration, what was reputed to be King
Harold's body was buried before the High Altar.

The more one makes research into the colossal
endeavours of Harold, the more one is compelled to
marvel.   After his decisive victory at Stamford
Bridge, that forced march, with a tired army, to face
the fresh peril of Duke William's invasion in Sussex,
may be counted as one of the pluckiest efforts ever
made.   It could hardly have been attempted with
any chance of success had it not been for the Roman
arterial roads that still ran so directly through the
length of the kingdom.   As it was, there was even
time for a few days' diplomatic sparring with the
'Tanner's Son' for negotiations before the grand
climax.   But Harold had a special affection for his
Royal manor of Wealdham, and even during that
ominously short pause found time to revisit the place
before going to meet his enemy.   He paid his final
vows at Waltham Church, where he supplicated fer-
vently for success against the invaders, remaining for
a time stretched out prone on his face before Tovi's
crucifix.   Believers in predestination and solemn
warnings will note that the figure of Christ was said
to have bowed its head as if in sorrow.   This inclin-
ation of the head might have been construed by
monkish chronicles into an act of assent to his prayers
if Harold had emerged victorious from the conflict.

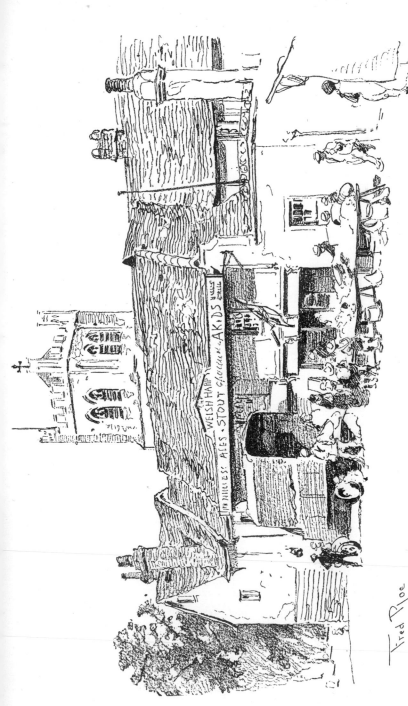

THE MARKET SQUARE, WALTHAM ABBEY

But it was not to be.   The ' last of our English Kings '
departed, accompanied by two of the canons of the
establishment, and that was the last that Waltham
saw of him living.   The fight which he and his army
put up against Duke William's disciplined host was
as gallant an effort as any handed down in history,
but nearly every one of the loyal Saxon warriors went
down in that tremendous conflict, and to this day it is
a mystery whether Harold's bones are at Waltham
Holy Cross or were left buried on the sea-shore.

Whatever the truth may be about Harold's splendid tomb in black marble which was said to have
been raised before the High Altar, it may confidently
be asserted that the grotesque ironstone mask which
was discovered amidst the débris of the ruins, and
now stands on a tomb in the present chancel, formed
no part of it.   The legend on this fragment runs as
follows :   ' Part of King Harold's Tomb, founder of
the Abbey,' but the style of lettering shows that this
could not have been inscribed earlier than the latter
part of the seventeenth century, while the object
itself—a product of the Renaissance—can hardly have
been sculptured as much as a couple of hundred years
previous to the inscription.

For generations controversy has raged over the
questionable date of the erection of Waltham's ancient
nave, and whether it is actually a fraction of the
building which Harold commenced or not.   If I were
to repeat but a tithe of the more able arguments used
on either side, there would be room for little else in
the present volume.   To me the massive piers seem
to belong to a more developed stage than the chapel
of St. John in the White Tower, built by the Con-
queror, and yet, with the exception of the clerestory,

are too simply Norman in character to date from the
enlargement of the monastery which took place in
Henry II's reign.   They undeniably emanate from an
earlier epoch than the vaulted passage known as the
' Potato House ', which is obviously one of the buildings erected during the second half of the twelfth
century, and is said to be built of Caen stone brought
over from Normandy for the extension of the conventual buildings.   The Saxons were not very ready
builders, and it may be that the progressive making
of Harold's church lasted well into the years which
elapsed after the Conquest, with such embellishments
or alterations as suggested themselves during the
course of time.   I believe that no documentary evidence exists that any rebuilding of the Abbey Church
took place in the years following Harold's death, right
down to the time when expansion was made in the
reign of Henry II.

Waltham's immense pillars, whether plain, chev-
roned or spiralled, are expressive of sturdy strength ;
but the developed beauty of the lighter Gothic, which
at one time must have existed in abundance in the
Abbey, can now only be seen unscathed in the Lady
Chapel, a gem of the Decorated period. A few poor
relics are gathered together in this beautiful building,
amongst them being the sounding-board of the old
pulpit, now converted into a table top ; a couple of
decayed keys from the Abbey ; some glazed Gothic
tiles ; a green glazed pilgrim's-bottle ; and the head
of a very ancient axe, which of course is conjectured
to have belonged to Harold. I think it is not generally understood that, contrary to the custom of
more modern times, many of the hafted weapons of
early ages were employed indifferently for husbandry

FIFTEENTH-CENTURY TIMBER HOUSES FORMERLY IN 'ROMELAND', WALTHAM ABBEY

Reconstruc.ed from Parker's drawing

or warfare. The same bills that helped to thin the undergrowth in Waltham Forest may well have backed up Jack Straw's violent endeavours on behalf of the men of Essex.   Finally we must mention among the relics an ancient thumb-screw, which can have had but one specific use.

Henry VIII's Commissioners did their work pretty thoroughly, and there is little enough left of the conventual buildings at Waltham. A double-doored gateway, of the fourteenth century, with a truncated turret ; an ancient span over the meandering Corn-mill Stream known locally as ' Harold's ' Bridge, but which dates from some three hundred years after the Saxon king's time ; and the damp, arched passage called the ' Potato Cellar ', from its sometime use as a storehouse for edibles : these, with a few crags of wall, are nearly all that remain. The pleasant meads bordering the Lea and its tributaries that were once covered with monkish buildings, and their gardens and orchards, now form a roving ground for herds of cows, which ruminate on some of the finest pasture land in the whole country.

In the market place, to the south of the Abbey Church, is an ancient overhanging inn, known as the ' Welsh Harp ', the main part of which dates from the fifteenth century. Beneath this building, running directly from the market place into the precincts, is a low broad passage, now open, but probably fitted at one time with a turnstile.   There is very good reason to believe that this building is a survival of the old Guest House attached to the Abbey, and that the thoroughfare under it is actually the ancient lych-gate, through which entrance was made into the cemetery.   Viewed from the precincts the effect is very picturesque, but the front of the 'Welsh Harp' towards the Market Place has of recent years been tidied up, in a somewhat painful manner, with rough-cast, which I, for one, would be glad to see unpicked, so that its timber front might once more be exposed to view.

The open space known as Romeland, close to the Abbey, still retains some picturesque old buildings, but the finest of Waltham's ancient domestic edifices were wantonly destroyed during the last century.

The Normans left plenty of evidence as to their architectural activity among the churches of Essex. The list is too long to be enumerated here, but amongst those possessing special features of interest are the little known, but very complete, Parish Church of St. Mary Magdalene, at East Ham, with its blind arcade and apsidal end ; the almost equally entire Parish Church at Rainham ; and that fine example at Heybridge, with its truncated tower, and the foliated ironwork on its south door, which latter decoration includes a clamp representing a dragon or sea-serpent. Much fine work of Late Norman character exists in the Parish Church of St. Nicholas, at Castle Heding-ham. Here, though the arches are still semicircular and simply moulded, the foliated pillar-caps from which they spring indicate an approaching transition to the Early English style ; yet the dainty stoup which adjoins the south door, and is a gem of Roman-esque work, seems to antedate the building in which it is enshrined. The vistas down the pillared aisles in this church are exceptionally beautiful.

The stately nave of St. Nicholas at Castle Heding-ham was built not many years before its tiny sister church of St. Peter's at Thundersley (that placid

TWELFTH-CENTURY NAVE,
CASTLE HEDINGHAM CHURCH

village with its terrific name), but an inconsistency exists between the two which is one of those curiosities of architecture so difficult to explain. The semicircular arches at Castle Hedingham undoubtedly belong to a less developed condition than the Early Pointed examples in the dark little building at Thundersley, but, on the other hand, the floriated capitals surmounting the pillars at Castle Hedingham are much more mature than those at Thundersley, which latter border on the archaic.

It is not a little puzzling to find so few evidences of the Early English—that purest of all styles—enduring in the churches of Essex ; but if the paucity of examples is remarkable, there at least exists one place of worship built during the First Pointed period, which, in some respects, is unique.

In that delightful little book of rambles entitled *Excursions in the County of Essex*, published in 1818, is a view of a building which, though horribly maltreated, still preserves an ecclesiastical appearance. This is specified as being ' Part of Coggeshall Abbey ', and the topographical artist seems to have enjoyed depicting it in its then picturesque but degraded condition. The structure stands on the Little Coggeshall side of the river, and now presents a very different aspect from what it did when Mr. J. Greig made his sketch. Disencumbered of the pigsties and stables which abutted on its walls, this building has been restored to its former dignity, though it no longer fulfils its original purpose of Gatehouse Chapel to Coggeshall Abbey. There has long existed a popular belief that the craft of brickmaking in Britain departed with the Romans, and was not revived until Tudor times. Numbers of pseudo-antiquarians adhere to this opinion to the present day. Yet the Chapel of Saint Nicholas at Coggeshall undoubtedly dates from the early part of the thirteenth century, and this material enters plentifully into its composition. The east and west ends are each lighted with three tall lancet windows, their long spare mullions being constructed entirely of moulded brick, as also are the angles of the walls. This brick is distinctly different in pattern from that used by the Romans. When in use as a barn, these lancet lights were blocked up to a great extent, but the obstructions have now been removed, leaving the mullions at the east end in a tolerably good state of preservation after the lapse of over seven hundred years. It is recognized that the fortified Gatehouses of Netherhall, near Roydon, and the Rye House on the Herts border (both of which are built wholly of brick) date from the second half of the fifteenth century ; but it would be exceedingly difficult to find another instance of the use of this material at so early a period as that at Coggeshall. Large portions of the domestic buildings of the Abbey remain, adjacent to and incorporated with the Tudor house built out of the ruins, and in many parts of these thirteenth-century brick may also be observed. Smashed up though it be, Coggeshall Abbey—or what remains of it—is by way of being a liberal enlighten-ment to students of medieval architecture.

NORMAN STOUP,
CASTLE HEDINGHAM CHURCH

9

CHAPTER X

OLD ESSEX CHURCHES—III

IT must have been the chance perusal of an old book in which was an account of a disinterment which took place at Danbury toward the latter end of the eighteenth century that first directed my attention to the antiquities of Essex. Though but a very small boy, the description of what was imagined at the time of publication to be the remains of one of the Knights Templars fascinated me. It appears that the Georgian gentlemen who were called in to report on the discovery positively gloated over it. The body in question was that of a comely, well-formed young man, embalmed and enclosed in a leaden coffin which contained a shell of elm, partly filled with a sort of pickle 'somewhat resembling mushroom catsup'. The parishioners and others 'satisfied their curiosity' with a certain lack of refined sentiment. They handled the poor remains rather roughly and tore off a piece of the linen shirt with which the corpse was covered, remarking that the fabric was 'not unlike Irish cloth of superior fineness. A narrow rude antique lace was attached to the bosom of the shirt ; the stitches were very evident and attached very strongly.' The more inquisitive of these investigators even went so far as to taste the pickle which the body was immersed in. Heavens, what a savoury ! A lot of irreverent damage

131

having been done, it is recorded that ' the leaden coffin was again soldered, and the whole left, as nearly as circumstances would admit, *in statu quo* '. In those pioneer days of antiquarian investigation it was rashly conjectured that the person so expensively interred was the original of one of the oak effigies in Danbury Church ; but our old acquaintance, Mr. Joseph Strutt, of *Queenhoo Hall* celebrity, thought otherwise, and, with more acumen than is displayed in the writing of his novel, subsequently made out a very fair case in favour of the body being that of the son and heir of Sir Gerald Braybrooke, who died in the year 1422, this being, roughly speaking, something like a century and a quarter later than any of the mailed effigies.

Danbury, both for beauty of situation and archae-ological associations, must be classed as one of the most interesting villages in Essex. The well-forested view visible from the Danish camp on which the church stands, and from which the place derives its name, is in no way inferior to those at High Beech or Laindon Hills. So lofty a spire as that which towers up on the elevated plateau can hardly hope to escape when tempests burst. Twice has the church been struck by lightning, and the catastrophe of 1402, which, according to Morant, destroyed the body of the building and half the chancel, was no doubt responsible for the horrific legend that the Devil himself had been seen walking about the church and behaving in an unseemly fashion. Variations of this fable are recorded by more than one historian. It is wonderful, considering the amount of devastation caused by lightning, that the celebrated cross-legged effigies of knights, for which Danbury is famous, have

EARLY THIRTEENTH-CENTURY
ARCADING, THUNDERSLEY CHURCH

been left to us unharmed. The figures lie under recesses, which may have helped to protect them : one in the south wall and two in the north aisle ; in each case the segmental arches which canopy them are supported by dwarf pillars, all of contemporary date. The effigies are said to represent members of the St. Clere family, who flourished in Essex during the reign of Henry III. Each of the warriors is clad in ringed mail covered with a surcoat, and there is a great similarity in their appointments, though some small but important details in the figure placed in the south aisle indicate that this particular one belongs to a slightly later date than its companions. The limbs of knights who habitually wore mail harness were apt to get uncomfortably chafed, and this inconvenience was not remedied till the latter part of the thirteenth century. Knee-caps were the first developments to be adopted, followed by greaves and elbow gussets. These additions were probably constructed, in the first instance, of boiled leather, and may be said to herald the advent of plate armour. The mail on the effigy on the south side is obviously fitted with knee-caps, which features cannot be detected on the figures on the opposite side of the church. A narrow examination will also discover that the shins of the southern effigy are protected by greaves. The omission of the mailed rings on the lower part of the legs has been supposed by some to indicate that the effigy under consideration was never finished ; but this is an error. Unfortunately, it is a matter of great difficulty to gain any proper view of these oaken figures. Against such necessary renewals as have been made to Danbury Church I have no complaint to urge, for they have mostly been well done. But why such peculiarly interesting survivals as these monuments should have been almost completely obscured by the placing of modern pews immediately in front of them passes comprehension. Surely such

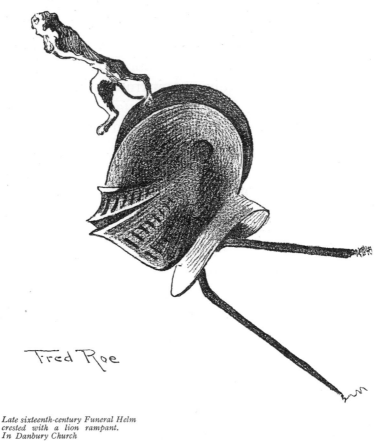

Late sixteenth-century Funeral Helm
crested with a lion rampant.
In Danbury Church

an unfortunate piece of arrangement could have been avoided as regards the furniture.

Two outstanding details of interest should be noted before departing from Danbury Church. They are the Mildmay helm, with its rampant lion crest, *circa* 1600, on the east wall of the north aisle, and the delicious little twin fourteenth-century niches in the external west wall of the tower. The latter help to demonstrate that, whatever damage was wrought by successive thunderstorms, the bulk of the tower was left intact.

It has been stated that, with the exception of the oaken figures enumerated in the preamble to Chapter VIII of this work, the effigies which Essex possesses are few and unimportant. This assertion can be successfully challenged. The number of effigies in stone, alabaster and marble, both recumbent and otherwise, is immense, and many of these are not only of very great archaeological interest, but also of a high order of excellence. Among the more prominent may be mentioned the splendid tombs of the Marneys, at Layer Marney; the recumbent effigies of the De Veres, Earls of Oxford, at Earl's Colne Priory, and Hatfield Broad Oak; those of the Wentworth-Howards at Wethersfield; the Maynards at Little Easton; the Fitzwalters at Little Dunmow; the Bourchiers at Halstead; the Petres at Ingatestone; the Earls of Sussex at Boreham; the Poyntzs at North Ockenden, and the sumptuous monument to Lord Rich at Felstead. Of kneeling effigies on wall-tablets the number is legion.

The fine but somewhat over-restored church of St. Andrew at Halstead contains two stone monuments to members of the ancient family of Bourchier, one of which is doubly interesting for a collateral article of the utmost rarity, which often escapes notice. The effigies of two knights and their ladies lie in the south aisle, those to the westward reposing on a table tomb under an elaborate multi-cusped canopied arch of late fourteenth-century work, the structure being profusely decorated with shields, mostly blank, though others are disfigured. The effigies represent Sir John Bourchier, K.G., Lord Bourchier, who died in 1400, and his wife, Elizabeth, daughter of Sir John de Coggeshall. On the wall beneath the canopy hangs a knightly shield, charged with the arms of Bourchier: *Argent a Cross engrailed gules between four Water Bougets Sable.*

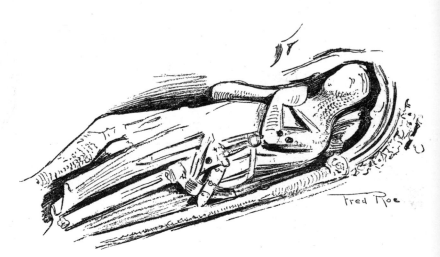

Recumbent Effigy of John de Bourchier, Justice of the King's Bench, died 1328. In the Parish Church of St. Andrew, Halstead. On the arm and sword sheath are slots for attachment of the shield illustrated opposite

To the eastward of the canopied tomb, but on a lower level, are two recumbent figures of earlier date, these representing John de Bourchier, Justice of the King's Bench, who died in 1328, and his wife, Helen de Colchester. On the left arm of the man are three deep slots, the positions of which correspond exactly with the staples which fasten the shield to the wall. The targe itself, which is kite-shaped, is an actual war-shield, a personal attribute and not merely an

article of pageantry.   There is not the slightest doubt
that we have here a piece of war harness dating from
some time in the first quarter of the fourteenth century,
it being well known that funeral effigies were fre-

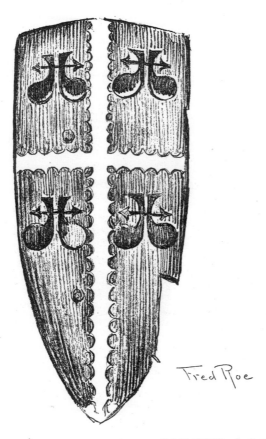

*Knightly Shield bearing the Bourchier Arms,
in Halstead Church*

quently executed during the lifetime of those whom
they were supposed to represent.

This is an almost unique instance of a war-shield
of wood being affixed to a stone effigy.   It should be
mentioned that the engrailed cross with which the
coat is charged has ignorantly been gilt in modern

times, which not only falsifies the Bourchier tinctures, but makes false heraldry.

Of the eminence of the Bourchiers in olden times a good deal of evidence endures. There are manors of the name in several parishes of Essex, such as

Bell-ringers' Cruse, dated August 23, 1658, in Halstead Church

Rivenhall, Coggeshall, Feering and Oldham, in some of which traces of ancient manor houses may still be found.

Another curious relic retained in Halstead Parish Church is the enormous gotch, or cruse, of black glazed ware, scored with a rhyming inscription and

THE COURTYARD, SOUTHFIELDS, DEDHAM

bearing the date AUGUST 23 1658. This was intended for the ringers' potations, and is now placed for safety in a locker in the belfry. A gotch of somewhat similar proportions, entitled the ' Braintree Fountain ', may be seen in Colchester Museum, and another of smaller dimensions, but of earlier date, is in the Parish Church of Marks Tey.

Some three miles north-west of Halstead the hawks of Hawkwood still disport themselves (in stone) on the tower of the Parish Church of that so prettily named village, Sible Hedingham. It is not necessary to go into the history of Sir John Hawkwood, whose punning device this was ; sufficient it is to say that he was one of the most famous *Condottieri* who ever took mercenary pay, or stuck true to his salt—while the pay lasted. Some say the church was built by him, but this can scarcely be. Hawkwood, the son of a tanner in affluent circumstances, was born in 1320 ; and though the fabric of the church does mostly date from the fourteenth century, the earliest portions of it must have been put up when Hawkwood was only twenty years of age. But that he contributed to its later enlargements there is every reason to believe. The tower in which the hawk devices are incorporated was a good deal remodelled in the early part of Henry VIII's reign, though much of the older material was re-used, amongst it being the Hawkwood rebus.

A sadly dilapidated monument to his memory in the south aisle of the church appears to have been smashed up by iconoclasts in the seventeenth century.

It was not only the mailed leaders of feudal hordes who were anxious to raise churches in expiation of

their violent deeds, or as begging petitions for the
repose of their souls. The Merchant Princes and
Adventurers who not infrequently financed these overlords were apparently just as ready to do the same,
and when they did not actually found chantries or
build churches they often enlarged and endowed
them.   Let us take two representative cases—Brightlingsea, at the mouth of the Colne river, and Dedham,
on the Stour.   A line drawn directly northward from
Brightlingsea touches Dedham, ten miles distant, in
the heart of Constable's Country.   Dedham, now a
quiet, sleepy, and very picturesque little town, was,
in the fifteenth and sixteenth centuries, a prosperous
market centre for the woollen trade, under the suprem-
acy of the affluent family of Webbe, cloth manufac-
turers.   A portion of their factory still exists in the
picturesque quadrate of half-timber buildings enclosing a still more picturesque courtyard, known locally
as the Old Bay and Say Mill.   The Webbes must
have carried on (for those days) an enormous business :
their resources were so great that they entirely rebuilt
the Parish Church, leaving it as it remains to this
day, with their merchants' marks in evidence on
various portions of the building.   A passage-way
runs under the west tower, the plinths of which are
decorated with panels of flint inlay enclosing the
crowned M : initial of the Virgin Mary, to whom the
church is dedicated.   In many ways Dedham Church
approaches more nearly to the type of structure
prevalent in Norfolk than any other ; its noble tower,
a conspicuous feature in the landscape, is faced with
that most indestructible of materials, flint, with
quoinings of stone, while brick enters but scantily
into the composition of the body of the church.

THE VALLEY FARM, FLATFORD

10

Throughout, the architecture is uniformly in the Perpendicular style.

A marble tomb, erected to the memory of the founders, dating from the early years of the six-

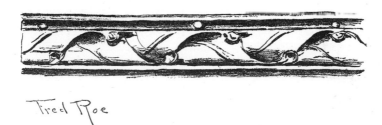

Running ribbon pattern on exterior of the 'Marlborough Head' Hotel, Dedham

teenth century is in the north aisle, and on the south side of the sanctuary is that curious brick arch with a flue running up one of the buttresses which has been

Foliated carving on the main beam of the ceiling to the dining-room, the 'Marlborough Head' Hotel, Dedham, late fifteenth century

the subject of so much antiquarian discussion. Dedham lies in a hollow, and any view of the town from the surrounding hills can hardly fail to include the church tower so reminiscent of Constable's pictures. And whatever weather happens to reign when you

visit the pleasant water-meadows between this town
and Flatford, the curious luminous atmosphere which
that great English master of landscape painting
managed to instil into his works is always visible.
I know of no other part where quite the same aerial
quality exists. If one had no previous knowledge
that Constable had worked about here, the mental
reminder of his vision would yet prevail.

Evidences of Dedham's former prosperity are still
visible. The 'Marlborough Head' Hotel, dating
from the end of the fifteenth century, was in bygone
days a Market Hall or Weigh House, with an open
arcade on two sides of its ground floor. The wealth
of carved beams in this hostelry is remarkable ;
they may be classed among the finest specimens
in the country, which goes some way to demonstrate
the thoroughness which existed here—for our old
market halls were often but indifferently decorated
structures. The courtyard of the 'Sun' Hotel contains one of those excessively rare features—an
external staircase. I know of only two examples
remaining in Essex. All along the quaint main
street are houses of late medieval and Elizabethan
times, Georgian houses, ornamented with cut brick,
and here and there remnants of beautiful pargeting ;
while southwards of the church, at the end of a leafy
lane, you come upon the ancient cloth factory of the
Webbes, looking rather forlorn and with its quad-
rangle overgrown with weeds.

Dedham is one of those old-world places where
really typical country characters can yet be seen :
hedgers, mowers, and ditchers, quaint people who
might have stepped out of some bygone age into the
present. A water frolic was in progress when I last

FLATFORD BRIDGE

WOLVERHAMPTON
PUBLIC LIBRARIES.

visited the little town, and the best swimmers in the neighbourhood were invited to compete for prizes, varying from eighteenpence up to five shillings. The whole of the adjacent population turned out to witness this event, and the scene amongst the barges and rushes of the Stour was indescribably picturesque.

Dedham Lock

An ambulance was in attendance, but no casualties were registered. Some of the heats evoked great enthusiasm, especially one which included a couple of stalwart ladies. The sluggish water near Dedham bridge rose perceptibly higher that afternoon.

To resume the subject of our Merchant Adventurers. In the main street of the old part of Brightlingsea stands an ancient timber house of remarkable appearance which you can warrant at first sight as having some curious history attached to it. Hump-backed and weather-beaten, it still bears up as sturdily as when it was put together some four hundred and fifty years ago. What we see of it from the street was actually once the back of the house, its front, which, architecturally considered, is not nearly so picturesque, being on the southern side away from the high road. In the north-west angle nestles a small turret of red brick, unmistakably Early Tudor in character and evidently an addition made subsequent to the erection of the main structure. So peculiar a combination of timber and plaster and red brick is remarkable. This house is called ' Jacobe's Hall ', and the stairway is known locally as ' Jacobe's Turret '. Who Jacobe was does not specially concern the present chronicle, but at the commencement of the sixteenth century we find that this house was occupied by the Beryffes, a family of opulent merchants and shipowners. What is left of ' Jacobe's Hall ', though not very great in extent, is sumptuous in its interior decoration, the carved and moulded beams of its ceilings being the finest of their kind. A mile or two away from the town, and situated on the uplands at a very picturesque turn of the high road, is the Parish Church of All Saints, the shell of which, though in part dating from the thirteenth century, was much enlarged and added to a couple of hundred years later. Like Dedham, the flint-faced tower has more of the character of Norfolk than Essex about it. The Beryffes undoubtedly contributed towards the expansion of the building. Listen to an extract from the Will of John Beryffe, dated August 25, 1521, relating to All Saints'

JACOBES HALL, BRIGHTLINGSEA

From the drawing exhibited in the Royal Academy 1929

Fred Roe.

Church, Brightlingsea. The words ring out as if inspired.

'ffirst I bequeath my soule to Almightie God . . . and my body to be buried within the Church of Brightlyngseay aforesaid. Item I bequeath to the high aulter for my tithes forgoten XX s. Item I bequeath to Bryghtlyngsey Church towards lengthing to our Lady Chapell according to the Chauncell III quarters of the ship called the Trinitie if God send her well home. And if she come not well home which God forfende then I give and bequeath to Bryghtlyngsey Church XL^{li} sterling to the use aforesaid out of the Barbara and the Mayflower if God sent them well home.'

This Will can hardly have been written by a man of law ; the simplicity of its wording is noticeable, the bequest of XXs 'for my tithes forgoten' being really quite good.

Presumably some or all of the ships did come ' well home ', for in the opinion of competent architectural authorities the said Lady Chapel, on the north side of the Chancel, was lengthened towards the east somewhere about the date of John Beryffe's bequest. And so it remaineth unto this day, with the merchants' marks of the Beryffe family visible on the sculptured shields which are ranged along the external plinth. It appears that these industrious traders had more than one mark for their merchandize, the earlier incorporating the black letter b in its design, and the later variety terminating in two angular tails. Both of these devices are incised on the family brasses in the North Chapel, which was enlarged by the bequest of John Beryff in 1521. The earlier mark, which is charged on a shield, is on the brass of John Beryff,

senior, 1496, which exhibits effigies of himself, his
three wives, five sons, four daughters, and two groups
of children. The second merchants' mark—that on
a roundel—appears on the brass of John Beryff, 1521
(whose Will we have mentioned), which shows figures
of himself and two wives, four sons and one daughter.
Another relic which may have had some connexion
with the family is the ancient barrel-lidded coffer
which stands in the chapel. Approximating in date

*Merchants' marks of the Beriffe
family in Brightlingsea Church*

to the Will, it might formerly have been used to
contain the documents relating to their benefactions.
    The Beriffes (as they eventually elected to spell
their name) continued to flourish at Brightlingsea till
the latter part of the sixteenth century. The family
was armigerous and prolific. One of the last of them
to whom monuments were shaped had by Anne, his
wife, eleven sons and three daughters. (There were
giants in those days.) But somehow one suspects
that their fortunes were on the wane. The last brass
in Brightlingsea Church which exhibits a ruffed and

befurred civilian of the name is that of 'William
Beriffe of Jacobes', 1578, after which there are no
more monuments to the family.   Perhaps their ships
did not continue to come 'well home'.   We hear of
a family bearing the same name, residing in Colchester
in the seventeenth century, but they figure as bene-
factors at Brightlingsea no more.

CHAPTER XI

ABOUT OLD ESSEX CHURCHES—IV

IN medieval ages the reaches of the Lower Thames can scarcely have been easy to negotiate. A deficiency of bordering heights on which such feeble lighthouses as the time possessed could be effectively placed, combined with the shallow and winding nature of parts of the channel, must have caused many vessels engaged in the maritime and coasting trade to ground and ultimately to become obstacles in the way of navigation. Thus it was that when a church was built on lofty ground commanding the estuary, like that of Fobbing, the tower was often used for the double purpose of a *pharos* and a look-out, or watch-turret. Fobbing lies little more than a mile to the north-east of Corringham, whose Norman tower was described in Chapter VIII, and is situated on the summit of an acclivity that commands an extensive view over the marsh-land, which in former ages was infested with smuggling gangs, and inhabited by a scattered population who were intermittently martyrs to fen-ague. Even in the murk of a foggy twilight a flare from Fobbing's elevated beacon could hardly fail to be noted at some distance, while on a good day you may see the church tower rising over the Essex flats from as far off as the Kentish hills, on the other side of Thames Haven.

There is a peculiar beauty attaching to these

venerable churches overhanging the sedge-dotted
marsh-lands which is rarely met with elsewhere.
It may be that their environment assists to preserve
their ancient aspect and protect them from the over-
zealous restoration which too often accompanies easy
access or wide popularity.   Fobbing Church, besides

Fifteenth-century Timber Porch,
Fobbing Church

its west tower, which dates from the junction of the
fifteenth and sixteenth centuries, embodies many
features of great architectural interest in its structure.
The beamed roofs of the chancel, nave, and south aisle
all belong to the fifteenth century, and the south
porch, a gem of carved timber-work dating from rather
later in the same period, nearly approaches that of
Margaretting for excellence.   Among the many fitted

items retained in the church are some old bench-ends, carved with pointed arcades, dating from the commencement of the sixteenth century, rare survivals of the simpler form of seating of that epoch. In the north wall of the chancel is an incised stone, bearing an inscription in Lombardic capitals of the fourteenth century, requesting prayers for the soul of one Thomas de Crawdene. The words, which are in old French, rhyme crudely.

✠PUR : LAMVR : IESV : CRIS /T :
PRIEZ : PVR : SA : ALME : KI : /CI : GIST :
PATER : NOSTER : /ET : AVE
THOMAS : DE : CRA /WEDENE : FUT : APELLE

Picturesque ' bits ' abound about Fobbing's straggling street, and the ' White Lion ' Inn with several other houses bear evidences of very early origin. The breezy village is quiet enough now, and very unlike what it must have been on a certain day in 1381, when a ' vagabond priest ', a native of the place, who called himself ' Jack Straw ', headed a revolt of the Essex peasantry against the obnoxious poll tax. One commission after another had been sent down to enforce the demands of the State, but the men of Brentwood and Fobbing either expelled those in authority, or, more effectually, chopped off their heads. A local Priory of the Order of St. John of Jerusalem, which had just laid in a liberal stock of provisions, was stormed by the hungry rustics and everything eatable disappeared down their throats— as well as three tuns of wine. How the rebellion first carried everything before it, and was finally crushed out with much bloodshed, belongs to other histories than that of Fobbing. It is recorded, however, that on receiving signed promises of pardon the bulk of the hardy Essex contingent returned quietly to their homes. Be that as it may, those who acted for the Crown saw that Jack Straw paid the penalty usually meted out to agitators who unsuccessfully engineered rebellions, and, in spite of the amnesties which had been issued, there is only too much reason to fear that several hundreds of his unlucky adherents shared the same fate.

Little enough remains now at Fobbing to remind us of the Peasants' Revolt, but the body of the church certainly antedates this outbreak ; indeed, portions of the shell would appear to have been over three hundred years old when they looked down on the seething mass of discontent which expressed itself in so unequivocal a manner under the leadership of Jack Straw.

In winter time, when the winds are bitter, and fog hangs over Hole Haven, the network of half-frozen creeks and rhines, with which the Fobbing and Corringham marshes are intersected, is alive with countless myriads of sea-fowl and wild duck, an ever-moving, restless host.

Some very unusual and exceptionally interesting evidences of the devoted parish priest of medieval times exist in Essex ; such may be found at East-wood, near Southend, and Laindon, near Billericay, respectively. Eastwood Church is a rather dark, lonely little building, lying up a turning off the main road from Southend to Rochford. The building has been enlarged and altered during various periods and presents a conglomeration of styles ranging from the commencement of the twelfth century down to 1500. The roof of the nave is supported by king-

11

posts springing from tie-beams, a simple form much adopted by fifteenth-century builders. The north wall of the nave was originally the outer wall of the church, and when an aisle was added to that side in the fourteenth century, thus enclosing the north wall, those who made the enlargement were considerate enough to leave one of the Norman windows in the wall intact, with remnants of two others. The font is also a remarkable piece of Transition Norman work, sculptured with interlaced arches. Inscribed biers are not often met with. That at Eastwood, which is curiously Jacobean in type, is dated 1706, and must be nearly three hundred years later than the pre-Reformation example at Ridgewell. But the most curious feature in Eastwood Church is the priest's dwelling incorporated at the west end of the north aisle, a piece of fitted timber accommodation which speaks eloquently of hardships endured by the humble incumbents of the fifteenth century, at which period it was constructed. A section of the aisle, measuring superficially some seven by eight feet, has been partitioned off by the insertion of an oak screen, formed out of plank-panelling, with an embattled surmount. In the space enclosed a ceiling has been fitted, in which is a trap-door, giving access from the ground floor to the upper stage. The whole of this structure is lighted by a single narrow window which runs up the west wall through both stages. In this chilly and contracted enclosure, without any means of warming the atmosphere, and in semi-darkness, the home life of the parish priest must have been rigorous indeed. The ground-floor closet (there is hardly any other name for it) is entered by a depressed arch, and a ladder is the only means of reaching the

THE PRIEST'S LODGING
IN EASTWOOD CHURCH

upper floor, through the trap. The communicating door once locked and the ladder drawn up through the trap, the priest was at least secure from intrusion ; while if he wished to keep watch he had only to look over the embattled parapet into the obscure vistas of the nave and aisles, into which a fleck of pale moonlight might occasionally penetrate. Short of an actual prison-cell, a more uninspiring or restricted little dwelling can hardly be imagined.

Something of the same sort of arrangement on a larger scale exists at Laindon, the difference being that whereas the priest's dwelling at Eastwood is constructed as a fitting *inside* the church, that at Laindon, a complete erection of timber and plaster, is tacked as an excrescence against the west front of the building, above which rises a bell-turret, reared on one of those wonderful cross-braced structures of giant oak beams which are remarkable features in many of our Essex churches. For many years the priest's house, as it is called, was inhabited by a schoolmaster who carried on his vocation in the ground floor of his dwelling. It may be this fact that has given rise to the supposition that the annexe at Laindon was originally built for the purposes of a school-house, but granted that its date may be later than that of the queer little domicile in Eastwood Church, it is probable that it was put up for the parish priest. Besides its lowest room and upper story, the Laindon house possesses a garret in its gable. Both the ' priests' dwellings ' mentioned are used to-day in the capacity of vestries, though in the Eastwood example it is difficult to see how much in the way of changing vestments is to be accomplished, let alone storing them.

With the exception of the features discussed, and the roof of the chancel which dates from the end of the fifteenth century, there is not much to note about Laindon Church, excepting its elevated situation, which gives colour to the surmise that it may in ancient times have been used as a sea-mark.

The condition of most of the parish churches in Essex is good—indeed, some have suffered by having too much money spent on their restoration—but there are a few to which an application of some part of this overplus of bounty would be a saving and a godsend. The interesting little wooden church at Hazeleigh, a lonely and poor parish some three miles south of Maldon, was pulled down in 1922, through lack of funds to repair the building, plus a lack of public interest. The total length of this tiny structure amounted to about thirty-seven feet, and though bare and humble of aspect it still retained traces of Elizabethan work. If for no other reason, the scarcity of wooden churches remaining in England should surely have prevented such an outrage as its destruction.

A couple of miles or so to the south of Witham is the parish of Wickham Bishop, where on rising ground, marooned in heavy fields, stands the semi-ruinous church of St. Bartholomew. The building is picturesque in outline, and still retains parts of its Early English and Decorated windows inserted in the Norman walls, where much Roman brick is in evidence. The interior presents a sorrowful sight. A fifteenth-century stone font, of good design, stands derelict on a smashed and disconnected pavement; the ceiling is falling away, and through the half-blocked, broken windows the wind whines a melancholy cadence. This venerable but sadly neglected

Fred Roe

CHINGFORD OLD CHURCH BEFORE RESTORATION

building is not past saving even now, and it seems a vast pity that no steps should be taken to preserve it ; an omission that some day will surely be regretted.

The neat little hamlet of Shopland, three miles distant from Southend, consists of a few domestic dwellings, straggling along the edge of a grass-bor-

The Porch of Shopland Church

dered road, an old farm-house, and the very interesting church of St. Mary Magdalene. With the exception of its delightfully simple early fifteenth-century porch, there is not a great deal about the exterior of the sacred building which calls for remark. But once the threshold is passed—the threshold, by the way, being the adapted lid of a thirteenth-century coffin

—a delightfully unassuming and picturesque interior is revealed to view, reminiscent of the late Edwin Abbey's illustrations of clerical life. In the nave stands a noteworthy font, the bowl of which is sculptured with arcading, and other designs varying from Transition Norman to Early English in character, and a few old bench-ends, while set in the uneven floor are quantities of medieval figured tiles, and the mutilated brass of a knightly figure in camail and plate armour of the fourteenth century, said to represent Thomas de Stapel, Esquire, Sergeant at Arms to King Edward III, who died in 1371. This individual was connected by marriage with the powerful family of Fitzwalter, and matrices of shields in the slab, above the canopy, seem to indicate that the armorials of both families were formerly placed there. The arms of Stapel were *argent a saltire gules between four staples sable.* In Weever's time these shields in stained glass existed in the north windows of the church, but those originally on the brass had already disappeared. Some beautiful fragments of ancient glass still remain in the decayed windows of the church, but they are mere patchwork, belonging to different centuries, and the arms of Stapel are not among them.

I write of Shopland in the present tense, from notes taken some years ago, but the word has gone forth since then that the church has fallen on hard times, and it is doubtful if all of the relics herein mentioned continue intact. The roof is said to be unsound, and the floor in such a deplorable state that the Rector himself, ably assisted by a contingent of Boy Scouts, has been engaged in the task of repairing the floor fissures with stock bricks. Poverty of the district has compelled this amateur reparation.   Could not some of the horribly designed and in many cases unwanted memorial drinking fountains which arise periodically over the land be dispensed with, and the resources available for their erection be diverted to the necessities of such a laudable task as this ?

The population of Shopland decreases, slowly but steadily.   There is no licensed house in the parish —which may not tend to ameliorate matters—and if any of its scanty population require an alcoholic quencher outside their homes they have to tramp over ploughed fields to Prittlewell, a mile and a half away, to get it.

How many people have the remotest idea where Chickney is located ?   Actually, what is left of the place has been absorbed by the neighbouring parish of Broxted, which lies some three miles to the north-east of Elsenham, in North Essex.   Village there is none ;   a couple of antiquated farm-houses and scarcely a dozen agricultural labourers' lonely cottages contain the entire resident population of Chickney.   The church, dedicated to St. Mary, stands on elevated ground, and is difficult to approach, but it is one of the most extraordinary buildings in the whole of Essex.   To begin with, its ground plan is eccentric :   on paper it looks very much akin to the figure of an unsteady robot.   It is as though the foundations had been commenced without any previous setting out, and that if subsequent discovery had been made of a lack of symmetry, the conclusion arrived at was, ' What does it matter ?   Get along with the job.'   Replete with evidences of the rugged immature methods of our Saxon forefathers, this archaic sanctuary has outlived its uses, and is now

forlorn and desolate.   Its very remoteness may have
proved a protection.   A few insertions in the way of
windows of the thirteenth and fourteenth centuries
are discernible, but little has been done to this relic
of pre-Conquest times since the Decorated Period,
even in the way of fittings.   The principal of these
fittings is the font, which dates from the early part
of the fifteenth century, and is elaborately sculptured
with ogival arches, under which appear cherubims.
In the spaces between the crocketed arches are placed
heater-shaped shields, bearing arms, one of which has
been identified as that of Braybrook, while in another
the devices (minus tinctures) can only be surmised
as those of Fitzwalter.

Quite recently an appeal was made for the trifling
sum of £250, in order ' that Chickney Church should
be put in sound repair, so that it may remain to serve
occasionally the purpose for which it was built before
the Norman Conquest, while at the same time it will
be an example of the simple architecture developed
by the folk of the countryside '.   I hope that long
before these lines appear in cold print this wish will
be realized, and that tragedies such as those already
described may be avoided.

In an article on Chickney Church and its surround-
ings, which appeared in the *Evening Standard* of
August 10, 1928, the writer mentions the following
particulars :   ' The oldest inhabitant—a farm-hand
over eighty, who has worked all his days on the farm
where his father before him also spent his life—could
remember when the choir boys and girls were provided
with red cloaks by an ancient bequest.'   The writer
adds :   ' I found none who could remember the last
wedding solemnized there.'

I doubt if any county in England contains more *graffiti*, or scratchings, than can be discovered in the churches of Essex. If such idle essays are the natural concomitant of boredom, surely, surely some of the outlying regions of Essex must have been among the

Graffiti in Steeple Bumpstead Parish Church

dullest places on earth in the Middle Ages. Many of these scratchings are traced with care and attempts at fidelity. At Steeple Bumpstead they are to be found in several parts of the church, and include some exceptionally interesting items, such as the record of a marriage in 1385, and the profile of an armed head, wearing a bascinet, under which appears a camail of the fourteenth century, reminding one of the brass in Shopland Church. A puzzle occurs with regard to these two *graffiti*, for while there can be no doubt whatever about the period of their execution, the pillars upon which they are incised do not appear to have been erected till about the year 1400. Scratchings in Willingale Spain Parish Church include repre-

*Incised figure of Norman knight,
Colchester Castle*

sentations of a ship in full sail, some crossbows, and a bishop in vestments. But to my mind the most remarkable of them all (secular in this case) is on the wall of the newel staircase in Colchester Castle. Here we have a very faithful presentment of a mounted Norman knight, wearing a flat-topped helm, and holding his pennoned lance in rest. At Rayleigh, on the south pier of the tower arch are several extraordinary scratchings, including some half-effaced but beautiful fifteenth-century lettering, and, what is

rarer still, a stave of music.   A remarkable anomaly
of later date may be seen
adjacent to these.   Under
the tower is a beam which
once formed a support to a
ringers' gallery, long since
disappeared.   The front of
the beam is decorated with
strap ornament, and the
brackets which support it
have their spandrels carved
with the wildest travesty of
Jacobean Gothic ever seen.
Even in the seventeenth
century the country craftsman found it difficult to
divest himself entirely of the
moribund traditions of the
Perpendicular Period.   A
queer little ' dugout ' coffer
also remains in the south
aisle.

*Scratching on pillar in the
Parish Church, Rayleigh*

Those who are interested
in the stone rood-screens
existing in our parish
churches should visit Great Bardfield and Steb-

*Another Scratching on pillar
in the Parish Church, Rayleigh*

bing, near Great Dunmow, some four miles apart from each other, and compare the very remarkable fourteenth-century examples at these places. That such fittings should have been carried out in stone is all the more extraordinary, since this material was formerly so scarce a commodity in the county that in the church of St. Martin, at Colchester, the mid-chancel arch with pierced spandrels in the Perpendicular style was constructed entirely of huge timber trees. It stands to-day as firm a piece of work as when it was first fitted some four hundred and fifty years ago. The tower of St. Martin's Church is truncated, and ivy shrouds a good portion of its surface. The upper part is said to have fallen early in the seventeenth century, but the ruin may have been augmented by some stray shots from Fairfax's guns in 1648.

The minster-like glories of the parish churches of Saffron Walden and Thaxted have no compeers in Essex. They lie only about seven miles apart, and are in a class by themselves. There are certain superficial similarities in the buildings, both their exterior elevations being in the Perpendicular style ; but whereas the spire of Thaxted is contemporary— a stupendous effort in a county where stone is practically non-existent—that at Saffron Walden was not added till the thirties of the nineteenth century, being designed by Thomas Rickman, who wrote so well on Gothic architecture. There is little doubt that Rickman was inspired by the neighbouring example at Thaxted ; before he took the matter in hand the tower at Saffron Walden was surmounted by as ugly a classic cupola as anyone would wish to see.

One of the primary aims of fifteenth-century

architects seems to have been plenty of light for the interiors they designed, contrary to the custom of earlier ages, when, more often than not, ecclesiastical buildings were rendered dark by the very fact that they were prone to attack from without. It speaks volumes for the increase of security which must have prevailed during the period of the later Pointed styles, despite quarrelsome landowners and internecine warfare. It also spells something for the growing domination of the Church.

The interiors of the parish churches of Saffron Walden and Thaxted are instinct with light—that of the latter particularly so. And yet in the windows at Thaxted there linger many fragments of old stained glass—saints, scriptural subjects, tabernacle work, and an exceptionally beautiful little figure of an armed knight, wearing the camail and holding a lance and shield, the latter displaying the arms of Mortimer. This evidently represents Edmund Mortimer, last Earl of March, who is known to have enlarged the nave, but the glass panel in which the figure is included has been transferred to its present position from an earlier window than that where it is now.

In addition to the increased window space afforded by fifteenth-century builders, the glaziers of the period also understood the advantages of having a larger amount of white glass interspersed among their colours, so that even if the whole of the openings had been filled with pictured glass the effect would still have been considerably lighter than in previous periods.

The North and South Chapels in Thaxted Church appear to have been added about the commencement of the sixteenth century, and the exterior interlacing

12

in the latest style of Gothic, above the window lights in these chapels, is noticeable. Thaxted must have been a prosperous place in the days of the last Earl of March, and his great-nephew, Edward IV, for the cognisances and badges of that forceful monarch appear in various parts of the church, as well as on an oaken sill in the Recorder's House, an ancient tenement in the High Street.

Thaxted Church contains some noticeable oak fittings, among them being a font cover and case which completely enclose the baptismal vessel.

Arms of King Edward IV on the Recorder's House, Thaxted

This elaborate structure, which towers up to a great height, is crocketed and displays traceried arches in panels of late fifteenth-century design. Similar instances of complete font enclosures occur at Pentlow and Littlebury, the body of the case in the last-mentioned instance being entirely formed of linen panelling.

It may be added that the gargoyles which serve on Thaxted Church comprise some of the most hideous chimeras ever invented by medieval sculptors.

The Parish Church of St. Mary the Virgin, at Saffron Walden, is generally of the Late Perpendicular order of architecture throughout, though some few traces of earlier work are discernible. Stately as the

FIFTEENTH-CENTURY FONT COVER
AND CASE, IN THAXTED CHURCH

building is, it fails to give (to me at least) the complete antiquarian sense of satisfaction which Thaxted Church conveys. There is a somewhat excessively regular effect of flatness about the nave arcades and clerestory which its more varied and less restored neighbour rises superior to. Walpole described Saffron Walden Church as one of the lightest and most beautiful churches in England—which maybe it is—but Walpole liked his Gothic very uniform.

Of old stained glass in its windows there is practically none. Many brasses, however, are here, including one of a priest of the fifteenth century, in Mass vestments, but the number of those memorials which have disappeared during successive restorations is incalculable.

Thomas Audley, Lord Chancellor of England, the flexuous and exceedingly ' useful ' minister of Henry VIII, was the sort of man whose monument one would expect to figure conspicuously in Walden Church. He assisted largely towards the building of it, and before he died, in 1544, he left in his Will an expressed wish to be buried therein. Audley had served his Royal Master in some capacity or other under six different Queens, and, strange to say, had yet kept his head. A sumptuous table-tomb of black marble in the Italian taste was reared to his memory in the South Chapel, and the inscription on it is said to have been his own composition.

There are numerous other churches in Essex which it would be a pleasure to review, but the present work is not intended to be an exhaustive guide. So with these references to two of the noblest buildings in the county I will close this chapter.

CHAPTER XII

AN ESSEX MYSTERY

THE old-time Customs officer who feared nothing, except that the public service might suffer, occasionally came in for some very queer experiences. One such may justly be termed 'The Mystery of Kitty Cannom'. Issues of the *Cambridge Journal* and the *General Evening Post* contain accounts, written in the month of August 1752, of this strange adventure, which, though accredited as regards local action, must always remain something in the nature of a romantic enigma.

One squally day early in July, in the year mentioned, a small coasting vessel beat up the estuary of the Colne, and dropped anchor a short distance below Colchester. Ever on the alert, some Revenue officers noticed that several chests were being landed ashore, and promptly proceeded to investigate. A ' genteel young man ' of 'about twenty-five years of age ', who, speaking in French, gave his name as ' Mr. Williams ' and his calling as that of a Hamburg merchant, declared these chests to be his property. They were duly overhauled—all except one—and found to contain much jewellery and costly feminine wearing apparel. The remaining chest, a case of large size, ' Mr. Williams ' endeavoured to retain intact, declaring that its contents must not be examined. Suspicion at once deepened on the part of the Revenue men, both as regards the questionable coffer and its owner. ' Mr. Williams ' protested volubly ; he raved, he asserted that the chest contained the body of his dear, dear wife, and even produced what purported to be a letter from the King of France in support of his *bona fides*, but all to no purpose. The usual rough-and-ready method of procedure in such cases was to run an instrument through the package and then test for the nature of its contents. One of the Customs men, who had more respect for his duty than for the King of France, had actually drawn his hanger for the purpose mentioned, when instantly the quasi-Hamburg merchant (who wore a sword) intimated that if any running through had to take place the process would be effected on the body of the person who attempted to commit such an outrage. And yet the Revenue men were not dismayed, for, while ' Mr. Williams ' was forcibly restrained, the unpacking proceeded with methodical precision. And all the time ' Mr. Williams ', like the heathen, furiously raged. At length the last of the wrappings was unwound, when behold, the embalmed body of a beautiful woman was disclosed to view. Here was a pretty situation. Nothing daunted and still suspecting some trick, or worse still, a horrible crime, the authorities had the cadaver removed to the Parish Church at Hythe, where it was set up in the vestry, for purposes of identification. Not a few curious people availed themselves of the opportunity of gazing at such a spectacle, and all the time ' Mr. Williams ' continued to lament—which is scarcely to be wondered at. Methods in those days were not of the kid-glove variety, and little respect was shown to delicate susceptibilities. A further mystery was sensed and those in authority were determined not to be hoodwinked. The corpse was refused burial, but 'Mr. Williams', who was detained in the church (failing a more convenient prison), was allowed access to the vestry, where he apparently passed several days and nights in company with the dead woman. In Georgian days it was somewhat difficult to procure interment for a deceased person on whom an embargo had been placed. As some analogy to the drastic and insalubrious measures just related, it will be remembered that as late as 1816, sixty-four years after the events we are now dealing with, the corpse of Richard Brinsley Sheridan was formally arrested by a bailiff, who successfully prevented the removal of the remains for burial until a debt of £500 incurred by the great orator had been settled. No one knows how the Essex mystery would have ended if among the visitors to Hythe Church there had not arrived a certain benevolent gentleman who spoke French fluently, and showed an interest in the unhappy young man incarcerated there. His sympathy evoked a burst of confidence from the prisoner, who imparted to the stranger a narration which reads more like a romance from the pen of Cervantes or Le Sage than a prosaic description of an English domestic tragedy. His name, it transpired, was not 'Williams', neither was his condition that of a Hamburg merchant. Indeed, he was a *person of quality*, and some of these early printed accounts reported him as being 'Lord Delamere', son of the Earl of Rosebery—a conjunction of titles that does not seem to dovetail. (Later on, when evidence began to crystallize, the appellation of 'Delamere' was corrected to that of Dalmeny.) His version of the matter was as follows : He was born in Florence, and had never visited England till some three years previously, when in London he first met the deceased lady, who appears to have been some five or six years his senior, and fell desperately in love with her. They were married and during the intervening period had travelled much abroad. Failure of the lady's health culminated in a rapid decline, but before she died she left a brief written confession that her maiden name was Catherine Cannom (Canham) and that she was actually the wife of the Rev. Alexander Gough, Rector (Vicar) of Thorpe-le-Soken in Essex, her last wish being that her body might be buried in that parish. My lord was shocked at the disclosure, but endeavoured to carry out the lady's dying wishes, and would have done so but for the interference of the Customs officers. The body was embalmed at Verona, and after traversing France, it was placed on board a ship bound for Dover. On arrival another vessel was chartered to take it to Harwich, but owing to the roughness of the weather the second ship was driven farther down the coast so that embarkation had to be effected elsewhere. My lord protested that he had been entirely ignorant of any previous marriage, and in floods of tears he expressed his desire to be buried in the same grave with his lady.

The foregoing statement may be taken as verbally correct, since it appears to have been communicated to the Press by the brother of the sympathetic gentleman, who was probably some local personage. It is even said that when he was allowed a sight of the deceased lady's face the gentleman at once recognized the features as those of Mrs. Gough, *née* Kitty Cannom.

The Rev. Alexander Gough was at once communicated with, but he was transported with fury and proceeded to behave in so unclerical a manner that he threatened to run his wife's ' last husband ' through the body. It may be observed that there is a sufficiency of this sort of menace throughout the narrative. Anyhow the reverend gentleman and his successor to the deceased lady's affections eventually made matters up, and the Customs authorities by this time having had their suspicions allayed, the corpse was placed in a sumptuous coffin and transported to Thorpe-le-Soken, where ' both husbands ' attended the funeral in deep mourning. There are some unimportant discrepancies in the old quaintly worded accounts, but taking it as an example of eighteenth-century procedure and manners the whole affair, while being a trifle grisly, is decidedly enlightening.

The intelligence that an embalmed corpse transported from abroad was to be taken to the Soken district may not have tended to diminish the shrewd concern which the Customs exhibited in the incident just related. The region was notoriously a great centre for smuggling operations, and difficult to supervise. A cave still exists in the vicinity of Landermere, near Thorpe, which tradition points out as being aforetime a ' hide ' for contraband goods, and mock funerals were not unknown to the Preventive force, though in this particular case their zeal evidently led them to a wrong conclusion.

With regard to the projected probing of the coffer containing the body, a nonagenarian residing at Rayleigh, and referred to in a previous chapter, has related among the reminiscences of his youth how a very active smuggler, named Peter Wright, assisted by himself, had hidden under a mound some bales

THE WHARF, LANDERMERE

of tobacco on which no duty had been paid. The job was just finished when they were rounded up by a couple of mounted excisemen and interrogated. Nothing contraband was found on either man or boy (which seemed suspicious in itself), but the freshly turned earth gave them away. Out came the gauger's prod ; a quick thrust was made into the mound, and the pungent smell of tobacco on the point resulted in discovery and arrest.

CHAPTER XIII

OLD MANOR HOUSES AND DOMESTIC DWELLINGS—I

ESSEX is full of old manor houses of the smaller county people and residences of the ancient yeomanry, but many of them, such as Broad Oaks (or Braddocks), Tiptofts, and Colville Hall, are about as easy to find as the particular part one requires of the Law Courts, the Board of Works, or the new Offices of the London County Council. Some of these Essex survivals, by reason of altered conditions of life, have been relegated into byways and backwaters, to drag out their old age more securely than if situated in a suburban area—perhaps reduced and abbreviated, but otherwise little spoilt by the hand of the restorer, and affording valuable insights into the life and customs of the past.

I think that the old domestic life of English counties can best be studied in the smaller residences which remain rather than in those palatial mansions within which the overlords carried on their court, and which to-day are often but lifeless showhouses. The small landed proprietor who seldom stirred far afield, and whose domestic interests were so self-contained, strove to make his timbered or red-brick dwelling as comfortable as the resources of his time would permit. Though these abodes were necessarily less ornate in craftsmanship, their homeliness was that induced by

Fred Roe

GATEHOUSE YARD, HALSTEAD

everyday use, and not garnished for the sake of
effect. Let us take a case in point. The earliest
known type of country residence consisted of a central
hall with wings at each end, its ground plan being
something in the shape of a squat capital H, or half
the letter, i.e. with the tops of the wings eliminated.
There was only one storey in the centre, for the hall
was open to the roof, but in one of the wings which
was cut off from the hall, an upper floor was added,
for sleeping and rest purposes, called the solar. At
the other end of the house a passage separated the open
hall from the buttery, or kitchen quarters. Into this
passage the front door opened, and the passage intersected the house from front to back. Draughts of
air were excluded from the hall (more or less) by a
panelled screen, in which two doors gave access to the
passage, which the servants had to cross when bring-
ing in food from the kitchen. This arrangement still
survives in the college halls of Oxford and Cambridge.
In domestic residences the solar, or sleeping wing,
was placed at the opposite end of the hall to that in
which the buttery was situated, which plan was of
course not followed in the colleges, the living quarters
being distributed throughout various quadrangles.
There seems to have been but little variation from
this planning throughout the medieval times. If the
house was small and unimportant, the wall-framing
alone supported the roof of the central hall; but,
in the case of more opulent owners, intermediate
props supported the rafters, forming aisles as in a
church, at any rate down to the fifteenth century.
The sole means of heating was more often than not
a brazier in the middle of the hall, round which the
domestics slept on forms or coffers, for bedroom

13

accommodation was of the scantiest.   In later Tudor times these primitive arrangements seem to have been voted uncomfortable.   The great hall was to a large degree discontinued, and the unoccupied space of its open roof filled with rooms, which were often fitted into the old Gothic framing.   During these alterations most of the old oak buttery screens disappeared from the yeomen's modest residences, and they are rarely to be found intact at the present day.   In 1928 a specimen of unusual interest, from the West Country, was presented to the Victoria and Albert Museum, which though disparaged by some as possessing no ornamental features, is one of the most precious records which has remained to us of the internal fittings of an unpretentious yeoman's residence of the fifteenth century.   Dotted about all over the map of Essex are numerous houses of pre-Reformation times which have once possessed open dining halls; now partitioned into compartments by timber-work and panelling of Elizabeth's expansive reign.   The most wonderful of all these ancient residences is Tiptofts Manor House, near Wimbish.   The first quarter of the fourteenth century could not have been long completed, and the boy king, Edward III, barely settled on the throne when the aisled and pillared hall of Tiptofts was set up.   So here we have a very good survival of the internal arrangement of a substantial landowner's residence some twenty years before the Battle of Crécy had been fought and won.   But of these antiquarian rarities hardly any indication can be detected outside, for respectable brick of Victorian times has effaced the ancient external features unsparingly. Within, however, there are considerable remains of the noble arcading of the great hall, constructed of

oak trees shaped into columns, from which spring
braces to support the roof. The style of these columns
and their capitals antedates the better known arcading
in Shenfield Church by something like one hundred and
sixty years. The hearth was originally in the centre
of the hall, and no doubt the smoke escaped through
a louvre in the roof. Very probably owing to the
lowness of its windows, and the great height of the
open roof, combined with the absence of any satis-

Horham Hall from the Park

factory heating arrangement, the great hall was a
chilly and uncomfortable place, but a couple of
hundred years or more passed before any attempt at
amelioration was made in the matter. Then a great
chimney-stack was built somewhere about the place
where the open hearth had been, and this was carried
right up through the roof, displacing the louvre. This
addition was no doubt conducive to warming the
place, but it was unsightly, and spoilt the proportions
of the hall—yet there it remaineth to this day.

The manor house derives its name from the Tiptofts, an honourable and ancient family who owned the lordship at the commencement of the fourteenth century. They probably built the earliest portions of the existing residence, but would appear to have alienated it very soon afterwards, since Sir John de Wanton, who was Sheriff of Essex and Hertfordshire, was lord of the manor at his decease in 1347.

A very similar building of approximate date to the foregoing is Stanton's Farm at Black Notley, near Braintree, though here the open roof of the hall has been entirely filled in with a ceiling, the space above being used as a loft.

The vicinity of Wimbish is replete with antiquities in the domestic line. Broad Oaks—or Braddocks Farm as it is now called—is another manor house, ancient certainly, but erected over two hundred years after Tiptofts. Broad Oaks was built of red brick, early in Elizabeth's reign, and the change in its planning from the old Gothic methods is noticeable. The big central hall has gone, and the more modest living-room which has taken its place indicates that at the time of its erection the last vestiges of the feudal system were passing away. It is uncertain whether the present building was put up for the Mordaunts or the Wisemans to whom the manor was conveyed in 1561. The principal glory of Broad Oaks at the present day, so far as its exterior is concerned, lies in the stacks of clustered chimneys, and the unrestored north front, where a fine double-transomed window on the first floor looks blindly across the moat. Within the house some old panelling and doors remain, and a couple of fireplaces of late sixteenth-century date, both of which are on the first floor. One of

BROAD OAKS, OR BRADDOCKS FARM, WIMBISH

these has a classically designed mantel of stone, and
the other—a queer little structure of oak decorated
with strap and jewel moulding—is quite the most
diminutive old oak fireplace I have ever seen.

The interior of Broad Oaks is dark, and wears an
inscrutable air, partly due to the fact that so many

*Colville Hall, White Roding.
A typical country Squire's
house of the early sixteenth
century*

of its ancient windows are blocked up. The priest-
holes which once hid elusive plotters, among them
Father Gerard—the same who administered the oath
of secrecy to the Powder Plot conspirators—are now
inaccessible. Of the perils run by that indefatigable
schemer at Broad Oaks his autobiography gives a
vivid description.

Some distance off the high road from Harlow to that clump of parishes known as the Rodings (there are eight of them), secluded and embowered in trees, stands an ancient mansion known as Colville, or Covell Hall. Here we have a quaint and compact specimen of a squire's house of the time of Henry VII, almost untouched by the hand of the restorer. Although fallen from its former state, the building still exhibits many evidences of bygone affluence. The framework of the house is of timber, filled in with herring-bone nogging, shadowed in some places with ivy. In 1802 the whole of the exterior was plastered over, as the date, enclosed in a medallion, indicates, but the original construction appears in places where the plaster has become detached.

Hardly anything is known of the history of this interesting house, but it is certain that the family of Colville possessed estates in Essex from the fifteenth century for several generations. At the time Colville Hall was built the manor of White Roding, in which parish the house stands, was possessed by Humphrey Browne, serjeant-at-law, in right of his wife, Anne, daughter of Sir Henry Vere, of Addington, but there is no evidence that he ever lived here. Anyhow, from what remains the Hall must have originally been the residence of a family of county standing, though probably not titled. It formerly stood in the midst of a pleasance, surrounded by a wall, of which no traces remain except a handsome red-brick entrance gateway in the Early Tudor style, which now rises derelict and meaningless in a pasture field.

If Colville Hall had figured among the illustrations to an architectural publication about the middle of last century, it would probably have been represented

RED BRICK TUDOR GATEWAY,
COLVILLE HALL, WHITE RODING

in an unsympathetic woodcut or steel plate, T-squared and sandpapered up with all the features accurately made out. In short, looking, not as it would, but as it ought to be. As one sees the old house nowadays, occupied with the homely appointments of husbandry, one finds it difficult at first to grasp the scheme of the place, though it is at once apparent that several of its details are extraordinary. Two small staircases which lead to the upper floor are adzed out of solid blocks of oak, each block forming a tread. These most likely belong to the earliest type of inner staircase in use during medieval times. On the ground floor there is more than one huge ingle-nook, though these seem to be insertions of later date than the original structure.

It was on a sultry summer day, with the temperature standing at nearly eighty in the shade, that I first made acquaintance with the Roding district. I approached it through a gorgeously wooded road from the Herts border. After a long and hot walk I sat down by a little brook and rested. A long, fustian-clad rustic, with a face like a withered apple, approached.

' Am I on the right road for—Roding ? ' I asked.

The man stared blankly, and I remembered the Essex dialect.

' Roothing,' I amended.

' O'ah, yow keep strate on t'roight.'

I had a second spell of pedestrianism, through less interesting scenery. Presently another rustic hove in sight. He was doing something to the road, and to him I addressed myself.

' Whereabouts is " Covell " Hall ? ' I inquired.

The native's fish-like eyes regarded the ' foreigner '

fixedly. 'Never heard of un,' he said. And yet
there it was, undistinguishable from the high road,
in a clump of trees.

The Rev. J. H. Stamp, who possesses much knowledge of the county, has mentioned this solitary part
as the ' Rodings ' or ' Roothings '— ' a district of Essex
remarkable for the poorness of its soil, and locally
for the dullness of its inhabitants. In a word, if
Essex be the Boethia of England, the Rodings are the
Boethia of Essex.' Britton, writing something over
a century before him, expresses the following truly
funny opinion. ' This district, which appears to have
obtained its name from the river Roding, which runs
through it, is very fruitful, but proverbially distin-
guished for the badness of its roads, and the uncouth
manners of its inhabitants : in both respects, however,
it is much improved, and with regard to the cultiva-
tion of the land, is not inferior to most parts of Essex.'

The Roding region is not a rich one, and many
of its most ancient and interesting domestic buildings
are in an unsatisfactory condition, but there is much
to repay antiquarian research. In the Parish Church
of Margaret Roding is a huge ' dug-out ' oaken coffer
measuring some ten feet in length by twelve feet in
circumference. Its front is a complicated mass of
locks and hasps, and its double-sectioned lid is ornamented with splayed ends to the iron straps. This
veritable giant probably dates from the early years
of the fourteenth century, and weighty as it must be
the craftsman who formed it did not overlook the
possibilities of transport, for the coffer is provided
with a lifting-ring at each end.

Most experts agree that Newport in this county
possesses one of the finest coffers in existence, but

Fred Roe.

OAK CROMWELLIAN CHAIR, FRINTON CHURCH

many other church treasures, ranging from the fourteenth to the eighteenth centuries, remain compara-
tively unknown. And the museums at Prittlewell
and Saffron Walden enshrine objects which are unique
and priceless.

CHAPTER XIV

OLD MANOR HOUSES AND DOMESTIC DWELLINGS—II

TWO old mansions that stand in a district which not so many years ago was beautiful and rural must be bracketed together : Eastbury House, connected by unsustained tradition with the Gunpowder Plot, and ' Parsloes ' (or Passlowes), an ancestral home of the Fanshawes. They are within a couple of miles of each other, to the east of Barking Town, and one wishes that their lot could have been better. Eastbury House, a fine old red-brick edifice of the sixteenth century, with stacks of lofty chimneys, still remains one of the most justly planned and noble buildings of its period existing in the environs of London. It has been conjectured that the house was built for one Clement Sysley, who, about the end of Queen Mary's reign, had a fancy to leave his patrimonial acres in Kent and come to reside in Essex. From certain indications in the planning and architectural details of the mansion, it seems more likely that Sysley found the house already there when he came to live at Barking and bought the estate in 1562. Less than fifty years afterwards the Sysleys were all gone, and the neighbourhood knew them no more. They were followed by the Stewards, who remained in possession for about half a century, and

THE TOWER OF BARKING CHURCH

14

after that a succession of short holdings seems to show that the prosperity of Eastbury was on the wane.

In the first half of the nineteenth century the house had got into so neglected a state that the owner, a Mr. Sterry, was with difficulty persuaded from pulling it down altogether. So it dragged on for years, till factories and chemical works came to poison the country-side.

When I first visited Eastbury House it stood in the midst of fields (once a pleasance) and was inhabited by a farmer. Owls sat on the cobwebbed beams of the great hall—which in this case is upstairs—and six feet of water was in the cellars. The place looked woebegone, and on an overcast day its local sobriquet of the 'haunted house' seemed justified. Since the Great War conditions have changed : the old mansion is now literally surrounded with cheap cottages of the working-class type, and Eastbury House, repointed, and looking less forlorn than of yore, has been saved from ruin and handed over by the National Trust for the Preservation of Ancient Buildings to Barking, as a club for ex-Service men. During the development of the adjoining land some antiquated timber barns, dating from the sixteenth century, unfortunately were swept out of existence.

There is a connexion between Eastbury House and 'Parsloes' which will be mentioned later on.

'Parsloes'—or what little is left of it—is on the border of the parish of Dagenham. One wanders by what, till a few years ago, was a delightfully rural lane, which turns northward from the Rainham Road towards Becontree. Almost overhanging the railway line to Southend, and near to a crossing bridge, is a solitary, ruined brick tower standing in a farmyard. This waif is one of the last remaining evidences of the ancient enclosures of ' Parsloes ' demesne. A few yards farther, on the opposite side of the road, is an old moated residence known as ' Porters ', nearly facing which a once noble avenue of trees—now terribly neglected—leads up to the gaunt, ivy-shrouded wreck of ' Parsloes '. The little wooded turn of the lane where the overshadowed lodge still stands, and that decaying avenue approaching the ruin, all speak eloquently of a time that has passed. Here was formerly one of the seats of the Fanshawe family in Essex, it being mentioned several times in the celebrated Memoirs of Ann, Lady Fanshawe, wife of Sir Richard Fanshawe, Bart., Ambassador and Royalist, covering a period from the commencement of the seventeenth century to 1671. The building was originally Elizabethan, and its exterior is supposed to have once been very similar to that of Eastbury House. Its bays were lighted with mullioned windows, which looked out on splendid gardens of great extent. During his residence there William Fanshawe, founder of the ' Parsloes ' branch of the family, added a large panelled apartment enriched with carvings to the house which he had bought in 1619. In his day the country around was delightfully rural, and in no way vulgarized by proximity to the advancing East End of London. The westward drift had not as yet asserted itself, and for over two hundred years after William Fanshawe's death ' Parsloes ' remained the head-quarters of his family. In 1773 was born John Fanshawe, who some twenty-three years later entered the church. The Rev. John Fanshawe, a squarson, imagined himself, like Beckford, to have a pretty taste for architecture, and

Fred Roe

EASTBURY HOUSE IN 1911

proceeded to 'beautify' the old Elizabethan and Carolean mansion of 'Parsloes' with additions and sham fortifications after the so-called 'Gothic' style. Nearly the whole of the exterior was faced with a coating of brick in true Twickenham manner, and a library with a coved ceiling was added in 1814, as well as over twenty more apartments. All the old gables were hidden by sham battlements, and a great tower was erected at one corner. Even the chimneys were glorified into the semblance of turrets. These changes were so numerous that it is difficult to recognize in some early photographs which exist of the place the Elizabethan manor house of ancient engravings. The Rev. John Fanshawe, who effected the camouflage, had a youngest brother, Thomas Lewis, some nineteen years younger than himself, who in due time became Vicar of Dagenham. This gentleman used 'Parsloes' as his vicarage; he also bought up four of the carved stone fireplaces from Eastbury House, when that mansion was in a bad way, and had them placed in his own manor house. Fifty years after the fireplaces had been transferred to 'Parsloes' the neighbourhood showed signs of becoming impossible. The last occupant of 'Parsloes' was John Gaspard Fanshawe, who retired to London, and died in 1903, and the mansion on which so much money and labour had been expended was left to slow decay and ruin. Over sixty years of neglect have now done their work on it. Before the Great War this wreck of a once sumptuous manor seat was in a semi-ruinous state. The brick facing superimposed by the Rev. John had failed in many places, leaving the older and sounder Elizabethan work here and there exposed to view. These evidences of a former style are in smaller red brick with blind diamond patterns in blue. When I last saw ' Parsloes ' it was absolutely dangerous to enter the place. Gaping ceilings and dilapidated rooms—through which it is said a ghost walks—are everywhere, and the tower, which once contained a fine staircase, is now a mere shell, open to the sky.

Troopers' horses had been stabled in the library,

Parsloes in ruins, 1922

and ragged apertures in the walls showed where the Eastbury fireplaces were once inserted. Even on the sunniest day the ruin has a weird and eerie air. *Débris* falls occasionally, and the ivy which clings to the tottering walls whispers softly to every breeze.

Dagenham country-side knows the Fanshawes no more, but memorials still linger of their former occupation. The Rev. John of that name lies in Dagenham Church, a structure that was shockingly rebuilt in 1800, and in the chancel yet hang a seventeenth-century helmet and gauntlets, knightly trophies of the family. An ancient tabard which accompanied these relics disappeared somewhere about the close of the seventies.

I like to think that there is truth in the old belief that, in places where the great have dwelt, something impalpable lingers in the dust till all time. The environs of our great metropolis possess few sadder instances of debasement than poor ' Parsloes '. It is a clear case of an ancestral home being abandoned owing to sheer propinquity. A miniature railroad for the conveyance of bricks runs through what was once a gorgeous garden, and a trotting track occupies the park. It was here that Mr. Walter Winans had a sudden seizure and died in August 1920.

Early in the present century it was rumoured that a member of the Fanshawe family intended to restore the house and revive its ancient glories ; but this has not proved correct, and I understand that the property has now passed into other hands.

It is pleasant to add that, despite the desolation of ' Parsloes ', the ancient family of Fanshawe still retains its county dignity. Mr. Basil Fanshawe, who is Lord of the Manor of Bratton Fleming, Devonshire, and carries on the family traditions, has informed me that many of the treasures from the old Essex residence are in his possession. A considerable part of the land in the manors of Eastbury and Passlowes at one time belonged to the Benedictine Nunnery of Barking, of which establishment, besides the well-known Fire-Bell Gate, a few rubble walls and the noble tower of St. Margaret's Church are now the only remains.

On the former treasures at ' Belhus ', something

over six miles to the south-west of 'Parsloes ', I should much like to dwell ; but since the sale of the Barrett-Lennard property in 1923 the contents of the mansion may no longer be considered locally. Of all the precious objects which adorned the interior of that much altered Tudor house nothing fastened itself so much on the memory of the writer as the superb pair of Flemish gates which opened the way from the west porch into the hall. Evidently the production of a master hand, they displayed the finest style of design associated with wood-carving which that country produced during the Early Renaissance, and the original colouring was still bright upon their pilasters and linen panels. It is as though John Barrett, who built the original residence about the first quarter of the sixteenth century—or his successor—had arranged for the best craftsmen in Flanders to produce these fittings—though certainly they must have been removed from their primary position to grace the awful Twickenham Gothic façade which was added to the west front about the end of the eighteenth century. In *Excursions in the County of Essex*, published in 1818, we find the following comment on these additions. ' The mansion was altered and greatly improved (!) by the late Lord Dacre ; the decorations made from his own designs are extremely neat.' Yet all this tinkering about was done in spite of Horace Walpole's previous opinion, that he never saw a place ' so totally devoid of faults '.

A short distance beyond Aveley, in which parish the Belhus estate lies, is the village of Stifford, an out-of-the-way place, in the vicinity of which are some unexpectedly beautiful bits of scenery, besides a collection of seventeenth-century miniature cottages

of remarkably picturesque appearance. Of simple
cottage types of the humblest class one of the most
curious exists at Horndon-on-the-Hill ; it is so primitive in its construction that I hesitate to place a date
on its origin.   Beyond Stifford is Orsett, another rural
gem, where the timber gatehouse of Bishop Bonner's

Fred Roe.

17ᵗʰ Century Cottage ᵃᵗ Stifford Essex.

A gem of cottage architecture

palace yet survives. This little visited part of Essex
well repays exploring.
   Sandwiched   between   Maldon   and   Tolleshunt
D'Arcy is the parish of Tolleshunt Major, or Malger.
When the smash up of the monasteries came, this
manor belonged to Coggeshall Abbey. After a short
ownership by Thomas Seymour, afterwards Duke of
Somerset, the manor was granted by Henry VIII to
Stephen Beckingham, a landowner in these parts,

who presumably built what is known as Beckingham Hall, a semi-fortified residence, of which little remains except the red-brick turreted gateway and *enceinte*. The Hall itself must have been a very splendid building, if we can reckon from the gateway, and a carved oak overmantel, which was preserved till recent years in the farm-house standing within the enclosure. This building is too small and trivial ever to have formed the principal part of Beckingham's mansion, but it may have been a subsidiary portion of the edifice. Some sort of tradition exists that Beckingham Hall was at one time destroyed by fire, in which case the overmantel may have been rescued and retained in the present house. The manor was bestowed in 1543, and the date 1546 appears (twice) upon the panels, as well as the Royal Arms of Henry VIII, and those of Beckingham, with their motto ENGRATITUD EST LA MORT. Three heads, sculptured in the peculiarly bold style of the period, are said to represent members of the Beckingham family.

While I was making my sketch of the place some commotion was caused by the hostile arrival of a large goat, which took exception to two or three clergymen who were gazing up at the entrance gateway. Butting right and left, the animal would soon have remained master of the field, had it not been for the arrival of a farm hand, in appearance the most picturesque descendant of Hereward the Wake's followers ever seen.

' Didn't yow hear me say I wouldn't have yow muckin' about here ? ' shouted this individual to the goat.

A battle ensued (with many regrettable words) which ended in a victory for this member of the ancient

.Fred Roe.

TERRACE ON THE HILL-SIDE, STIFFORD

Anglo-Saxon race, and the goat was hurried off, resisting vigorously.

The wonderful panelling at D'Arcy Hall, in the adjacent village of Tolleshunt D'Arcy, I have already described in another work.

All that is left of Nether Hall, the once splendid residence of the Colte family, is a ruined gatehouse, flanked with towers of a semi-fortified type ; and a

The Gatehouse, Beckingham Hall

loopholed wall guarding the moat. The existing remains are of brick (a fairly early instance of the use of that material), the colour being of a rich red, with geometrical patterns in blue. Round the summit of the towers runs a cusped arcading of cut brick—a sort of survival of the machicolations of earlier days ; this arcading is continued along the face of the curtain wall. The Hall is said to have been built by Thomas Colte, Esquire, about the year 1470, but it seems more likely that when he purchased the manor there was already a residence there. I venture to suggest that the latter may have been the very house which stood within the enclosure, and has now entirely vanished. Granted that the moat was already there, the gate-house and curtain wall which we now see may have been built as an extra protection to the habitation by his son John Colte, at the end of Edward IV's reign —or very soon after. The evidence of the badge of Edward IV on one of the corbels seems to me insurmountable as regards the latter theory.

One is more inclined nowadays to associate the name of Colt with fire-arms than with the somewhat coarse practical jokes which aroused such merriment with our forefathers. It was, however, Sir Henry Colte, of Nether Hall, a witty constituent of the Court of Henry VIII, who exploited that renowned *battue* of certain monks of Waltham Abbey, when they so far forgot the proprieties as to make their return from Cheshunt Nunnery rather late one evening. The results of the frolic, and the king's comment on it, are too well known to be repeated herein. Nether Hall stands in the parish of Roydon, off an unfrequented by-road. The ruin is gaunt and desolate ; but when the afternoon sun falls on those mellow walls, their colour glows a vivid crimson which it would be difficult to match.

Semi-fortified walls encircling ancient manor houses exist in good condition in many parts of Essex, notably at ' Killigrews ', near Margaretting, where is probably one of the finest specimens in existence, though the house which it encloses was squared-up and abbreviated in the early part of the eighteenth century. ' Killigrews ', unlike the wreck of the

Fred Roe.

THE GATEHOUSE, NETHER HALL, ROYDON

15

Colte's mansion at Nether Hall, is in an excellent and flourishing condition.

Rochford Hall comes under the head of a larger class of mansion than those which have hitherto been considered. This ancient manor house stands on the edge of a pleasant green, and though lopped and shorn of its former proportions and dignity, is at once recognizable as having been the palatial residence of an ambitious family who have helped to make history. A flat, gabled façade, lighted by many Victorian windows which face out on the green, and a tall flanking turret still look imposing in that plaster-coated remnant of a fine house. Hardly anything of antiquarian interest exists inside the building, but in the courtyards a few Tudor arches and windows—spared by nineteenth-century subverters—yet remain to show what its pristine features were like. The demesne was at one time in the possession of the Boleyn family; but in spite of a persistent tradition to that effect, it seems altogether improbable that Anne, Henry VIII's second queen, was born at Rochford. Anyhow, it is certain that Anne Boleyn could not first have seen the light in the building which at present constitutes Rochford Hall, since all evidence is in favour of the structure being conterminous with the latter years of Henry's reign.

The Rochford folk still possess a sense of exalted importance from their place having had some connexion with a queen. Once when I was lunching at the principal inn, the opening of a door released a babel of voices from the tap-room, among which the following priceless jewels were audible:

'This here's a town, not a village; it's called Rochford, which means the ford over the Roach——'

A heated argument followed this statement.—' And Anne Bullin, up at the Hall, ah ! she didn't live yesterday, she didn't. She was afore the time of Lloyd George, she was. You can't expect Almighty God to change the nature of things, you can't, so what's the use of argufying ? '

This and some remarkably trenchant opinions on female suffrage comprised the whole controversy.

Fred Roe.

STONE AND BRICK CHIMNEYPIECE,
EARLY FIFTEENTH CENTURY. DIS-
COVERED AT PRITTLEWELL; NOW IN
THE VICTORIA AND ALBERT MUSEUM

Fred Roe

$\begin{smallmatrix} & T \\ G & E \end{smallmatrix}$
1685

COLNEFORD HOUSE

CHAPTER XV

OLD MANOR HOUSES AND DOMESTIC DWELLINGS—III

U P to the present this section of my book has not assumed too cheerful an aspect, for there is an element of pathos about deserted or deteriorated mansions which renders the very task of writing about them a woeful one. But it is sadder still when every vestige of a once beautiful residence has disappeared, leaving only its name, perhaps attached to a roadful of small villas, as in the case of that exclusively oaken residence of the fifteenth century, Leigh Hall. It is more agreeable to linger over those old homesteads which are inhabited under prosperous circumstances, and have not been left to decay, damp, and slow ruin. Of all classes of ancient domestic dwellings which have declined during the last century or so, those decorated with parge work have perhaps been the worst sufferers. There is no county in England where that form of exterior embellishment has been carried out more successfully than Essex. But nowadays, though certain simple patterns are occasionally hatched on plaster-work, all the art with which the pargeter's craft once teemed seems lost and obsolete.

Among the finest specimens of such ornamentation is that on Colneford House, at Earl's Colne, a charmingly picturesque residence standing behind an old wall, on the side of the road near Pound Green. Colneford House was probably built in Elizabethan times, as the huge red-brick chimney-stack testifies, but it was brought up to date and the façade decorated with elaborate pargeted patterns in 1685, which year is recorded on its front in a cartouche, with the accompanying initials $_G^T{}_E$. In the seventeenth century Colneford House appears to have been in possession of the Toller family, and the initials mentioned have been identified with George and Elizabeth of that name. Though the building is nearest the village of White Colne, the boundary separating the parish from that of Earl's Colne crosses its south-west wing. Mrs. Wren, O.B.E., in an interesting article in *The Connoisseur*, has related an anecdote which I will repeat in her own words. ' This junction of the parishes led to an amusing episode in which the Vicar of White Colne, who was then living in Colne Ford House, scored off his parishioners. The latter protested strongly at his living out of the parish, and begged him to take immediate steps to change his abode. The Vicar readily assented and—moved his bed into the adjacent room.' This occurred in 1724, and the boundary is duly marked by a leaden plaque bearing the date, which remains to this day.

I know of no more fascinating and exquisite specimen of an old English residence than Colneford House, its beauties retiring behind a mass of trees, and its late seventeenth-century gateposts and enclosing walls mottled with lichen. The place possesses a subtle sense of attraction, while apparently seeking to withdraw itself from public notice.

The neighbourhood of the Colne Valley is full of good things, and it is possible to find the *molet* of the

THE GATEWAY, COLNEFORD HOUSE,
EARLS COLNE

WAKE COLNE

De Veres in evidence on many half-timbered and plastered houses, as it is on the summit of the tower of Earl's Colne Parish Church, speaking of times when the mighty Earls of Oxford ruled in that part of the land.

The intricately patterned house at Wivenhoe, some forty or fifty years earlier in date than Colneford House, is much more widely known, but though justly admired by every one seemed only a few years ago to be threatened with extinction. I first saw that wonderful specimen of the pargeter's art on a stormy day when the very skies seemed to weep that so fine a specimen of domestic work should be abandoned to such neglect and degeneracy. The windows were boarded up, and down the moulded scrollwork on its walls poured streams of water from defective gutters. All this is now remedied; the Wivenhoe house has been well and carefully restored and bids fair to adorn the place for many generations.

'Crown House', at Newport, exhibits some good specimens of parge-work, of a later character and disposed in panels. This building, like Colneford House, seems to have originated in Elizabethan times; but the pargeted front was added in 1692, as the date over its shelled doorway attests. The house, of which a fleeting glimpse can be obtained from the railway line, is well known, and is such an object of interest that visitors often pass unnoticed the timber and brick-noggined dwelling known as 'Monk's Barn', in the upper part of the village. 'Monk's Barn' has one of the most perfect fifteenth-century exteriors left in the county; its coved centre, moulded pilasters, and projecting sill to the mullioned window above are excellent examples of mid fifteenth-century domestic architectural details at their best.

Doreward's Hall is in the parish of Bocking, and stands in the fields between the church and that wonderful array of sixteenth- and seventeenth-century houses known as Bradford Street. The manor house derives its name from the ancient family of Doreward, or Durward, one of whom purchased the estate from Richard de Bocking in 1316. The Dorewards continued to hold the manor till late in the fifteenth century, when the male line failed and Elizabeth Doreward became the heiress of the family. She married Thomas Fotheringay, and had three daughters, co-heiresses, between whom the Doreward property, amounting to over twenty lordships and capital estates, was divided. The second daughter, Ellen Fotheringay, married Henry Thoresby, or Thursby, a member of a family long settled in Norfolk, and their son is said to have rebuilt Doreward's Hall in 1579, though this detail is disputed. At any rate the place continued with the Thursbys until 1637, when the senior branch removed to Northamptonshire, eventually becoming identified with Abington. In 1736 the male line of this branch was extinct, but the name and arms were assumed by a descendant, John Harvey (d. 1764), from whom the later Thursbys of Abington, the Thursby-Pelhams, the Thursby baronets, and the Thursbys of Culverlands are derived. So also for that matter is my Wife, whose Mother could trace her descent from the marriage in 1770 of John (Harvey) Thursby's eldest daughter, Honor, with (Sir) John Burton of Wakefield, who was at that time a cornet in Conway's dragoons.

In Doreward's Hall may still be seen the carved oak overmantel dated 1579, bearing the black chevron and three ramping lions of the Thursbys, quarterly with the arms of five other families with whom they were connected—Fotheringay, Doreward, Coggeshall, Harsick, and another. This doubtless was one of the improvements carried out by Edward Thursby, but as regards the Hall being actually *rebuilt* by him I

Sixteenth-century houses, Bocking Street

can only say that the term must have been very loosely used, for the sixteenth-century portion of the house which remains dates from a somewhat earlier period than that specified. What is left of it is a composite structure of timber, plaster, and little red bricks, the quoins being simulated with plaster. The pinnacled buttresses at the south-west end of the building give it a curiously inverted appearance;

these are chequered all the way up in imitation of stone.

The south aisle of Bocking Church belonged to the Dorewards, and therein yet remains a fine brass representing John Doreward (d. 1422) in full plate armour of the early part of the fifteenth century, and his wife, wearing the fashionable horned head-dress of her day. This John was knight of the shire for Essex in 1395, and was returned to five later parliaments, while in 1399 and 1413 he was Speaker of the House of Commons. But that is almost forgotten in parts where nowadays Courtauld is the name to conjure with.

The ancient appearance of a prosperous rural community is admirably retained on the south side of Writtle Green, where a most delightful array of old-time residences clusters, of which ' Aubyns ', at the corner of the lane leading to the church, is perhaps the most picturesque. ' Aubyns ' possesses its old corner posts supporting the overhanging angles, the trusses being sections chosen from the branchings of some large oak ; but what is rare nowadays, the house retains on its ground floor several of its original windows, arched and with leafed spandrels. These formerly looked onto the lane, but now, with one exception, are filled in.

A very successful insight to the methods of ancient domestic life could be obtained by studying the various structures of three successive centuries existing in Colchester and Saffron Walden alone. There is sufficient education for the student of this branch of archæology in the run of timber dwellings which extends on each return at the corner of Myddylton Place and Bridge Street, Saffron Walden, to furnish

Dorewards
Hall.
Bocking.

Fred Roe.

Arms of
The
Thursbys

ANCESTRAL HOME OF
THE THURSBY FAMILY

'AUBYNS', WRITTLE GREEN

a whole volume of explanations. The original inten-
tions as to the *ménage* of the corner house and their
subsequent modification can clearly be made out.
Much of the original beauty of the interior has necessarily been lost by interpolations, but a certain amount
of information is gained as regards changes in habits.
The corner house itself retains a good part of its
screened hall, *temp*. Henry VII, altered to accom-
modate itself to a later style of living by the insertion
of panelling. The exterior of this part of the residence
has been plastered up, and every true antiquarian
would be glad to see the superimposed facing picked
off and the framing exposed so that it corresponds
with the continuation of the façade up Myddylton
Place. This part, at some time during the eighteenth
century, was protected from improvement (!) by
being turned into a malting.

The munificence of Mr. Noel Buxton, M.P., has
laid open to the public one of the greatest domestic
treasures which Essex possesses in the shape of Paycocke's House at Coggeshall. Of Paycocke's House it
is difficult to say anything fresh. The place has been
admirably restored, and now presents a specimen of
what could be accomplished by builders, joiners, and
cunning craftsmen in the art of wood-carving during
Henry VII's reign. The choicest trees of a forest
must have contributed to the ceilings, and the fanciful
carvings are nowhere to be excelled. How any such
proposal to pull down the place originated—as it
actually did in the nineties of last century—passes
comprehension. To disintegrate such a sound piece
of work would have cost more money than the
wretched tenements which would have sprung up on
its site were worth. Let that pass ; but I have heard

16

dreadful names for such people as those who con-
ceived the idea. Two things particularly struck me
about the interior fittings of Paycocke's House. One
was that the linen panelling with which it is furnished
showed indications of being executed at a later time
than that which adorns the great carriage gates in
the façade of the house. Another was a suspicion
that the master-craftsman who was responsible for
the carving on the ceiling beam and joists of the hall
must have been one who at least had studied abroad,
for the flamboyant tracery with which they are
profusely decorated shows a distinct foreign tendency.
Even more pronounced than the carving overhead
are the three traceried panels inserted among the
linen-fold examples in the East Room. The latter
are without doubt French or Flemish, but were never
intended for the position they now occupy. Paycocke's House is additionally interesting as being
designed, without any defensive planning, for a
wealthy merchant, and its many windows indicate an
assurance of security which was lacking in the residences of the nobles of the Flowery War. The house
narrowly escaped destruction by fire in October 1928,
when some oak panelling and chimney beams in the
Garden Room were burnt.

'Jacobe's Hall', at Brightlingsea, the ancient home
of the Beryffes, another family of merchant princes,
is referred to in Chapter X. Though less ornate in
character than Paycocke's House, this is one of the most
picturesque buildings in the whole of Essex—so quaint
and unusual that how it ever escaped destruction in
unenlightened times is little short of a marvel.

Much later in date than either of the last-
mentioned mansions, the 'Old House' at Clavering is

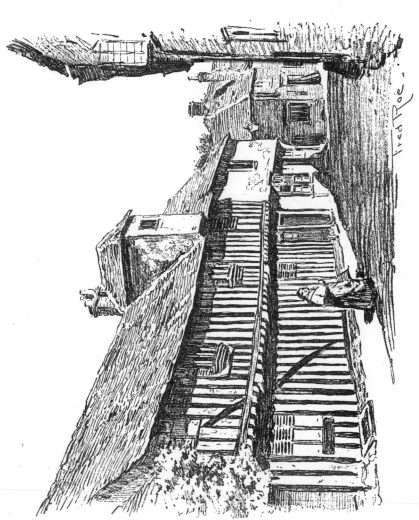

MYDDYLTON PLACE, SAFFRON WALDEN

BRIDGE STREET, SAFFRON WALDEN

chiefly remarkable for its frescoes and wall-paintings of the seventeenth century, a form of decoration not frequently found in this county. The well-preserved ' powdering closets ' on the first floor of this house speak convincingly of bygone manners and customs.

Old Guildhalls and Moot Halls have been so ruthlessly destroyed that very few of these relics remain

The Moot Hall, Steeple Bumpstead

in Essex. A scanty number of cottages may be found in outlying districts to which the first term still clings, but practically the only buildings which give any indication of their former municipal uses are at Maldon, Steeple Bumpstead, and Thaxted. The first rises over the houses in High Street, in the form of a massive red-brick tower, dating from the reign of Henry VI, and is sometimes called D'Arcy's Tower, from the tradition that it was built and presented to the town by Sir Robert D'Arcy, about the middle of the fifteenth century. The Moot Hall at Steeple Bumpstead is half-timbered on a brick base, and stands isolated in the centre of the village. At Thaxted, at the parting of the ways in the High Street, is the one almost perfect specimen of a

Thaxted

medieval municipal building remaining in the whole county. Its ground floor is an open arcade, with a little cell for prisoners tucked away in one corner. Under the covered space market transactions were carried out when Thaxted was a populous town, and a great centre for the woollen trade ; but it is silent now and deserted, except when used as a playground by a few small children. The timber framing of

Thaxted Guildhall is simple but effective, and the clustering of the brackets supporting its overhanging first floor very graceful. The building backs on to a jumble of old timber dwellings dating from the fifteenth century—approximately the same age as the Guildhall—and the whole environment is so quaintly bygone

Early sixteenth Timber House,
Newbiggin Street, Thaxted

that the presence of a figure in modern costume jars upon the imagination.

Not far from the Guildhall stands the 'Recorder's House', another fifteenth-century relic, with the arms and badges of Edward IV carved on its window-sills; while in several of the houses in the quiet little town the Bourchier knot may be found on the moulded ceiling beams.

Buildings which bear marks or badges connecting them with the ancient trade guilds are excessively scarce. At Witham, in the Bridge Street end of the town, is an early sixteenth-century half-timbered house with carved brackets, on one of which is represented a glove. It may be that this device had some affinity with the glove-making industry which is said to have

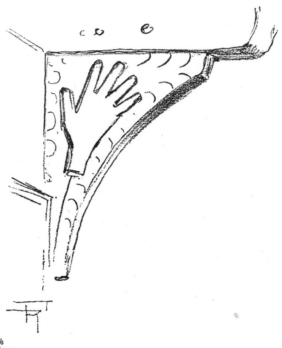

Bracket carved with
Glovers' sign, Witham

existed here formerly, though what trades certain other figures on the woodwork are intended to typify it would be hard to say.

Faulkbourne Hall, for two hundred and sixty years the seat of the Bullock family, and the remains of the White Canons' Abbey at Beeleigh, are among the gems of the county, but their architectural features are too well known to be detailed here. The former, like so many Essex mansions, is constructed entirely of red brick, but has never undergone any vicissitudes; while what was not pulled down at Beeleigh during the Reformation became at one time so degraded that cattle and swine herded in the Chapter House and Chapel. All this has long been altered, and under the tenancy of Mr. R. E. Thomas the building is now one of the most tastefully restored specimens of its kind.

CHAPTER XVI

THE FOREST

WHAT is known nowadays as Epping Forest is—with the scanty patches of that of Hainault—the last remains of the Great Forest of Waltham. The residue which has fortunately been preserved to us is only a tithe of its former size, but it is yet sufficiently large to get uncomfortably lost in. Oak trees of great bulk are inconsiderable in numbers, but the hornbeam, the beech, and the elm flourish in abundance. In parts such as Ambresbury Banks it is often difficult to see the sky when amongst the thickets, and underfoot is a primeval carpet of fallen leaves centuries upon centuries old. On summer afternoons when the shadows lengthen and the glades grow cool, in contrast to the Western sun which gilds the tree-tops, Epping Forest is lovely indeed. Silence is only broken by the low hum of insects. And here we are at a disadvantage, for peaceful resting in the forest is at times rendered difficult owing to mosquitoes. Deep down in the dells lie innumerable little ditches and shallow pools of water where the larvae hatch, and from whence these pests issue to make life irritating. I have often marvelled, not at the violent tempers of such knights of the road as frequented the locality, but at their unwearied attention to business in spite of these

IN EPPING FOREST

Fred Roe

distractions.   Turpin, and the Waltham Blacks, all must have experienced the scourge.

But what about the Waltham Blacks?

In the first half of the eighteenth century a certain Captain Johnson took upon himself the task of compiling a history of the lives of highwaymen and robbers, and his account of the Waltham Blacks may be taken as fairly correct, since the break-up of the gang only occurred a few years before his book saw the light in cold print.   According to Captain Johnson this band described itself as a 'nation', under the leadership of Prince Oronoko, who was 'King of the Blacks'.   They hunted deer in the moonlit glades of the forest, and did not stop short of taking human life if they were attacked, though in other respects they seem to have been rather a rollicking set of fellows.   Johnson was assisted in his description of the gang by a letter, which he received from a gentleman who was forced by the lameness of his horse to stop one night at a small ale-house in the forest, and was discovered there by a party of men with blackened faces, to his great uneasiness.   Luckily for this individual, whose name has not come down to us, the freebooters were in a merry mood that evening, and after some absurd ceremonies they invited him to join them at their supper, which consisted almost entirely of venison.   They informed the benighted traveller of their rules, but apparently did not swear him in as a member of their fraternity—one condition being that no person was eligible until he had been twice drunk, so that they might be perfectly acquainted with his temper.   About two o'clock in the morning the company broke up, after informing their unwilling guest that they would be happy to see

him at supper any Thursday evening. Quite a satisfactory termination to an Early Closing Day's somewhat risky adventure.

The Waltham Blacks were eventually appre-
hended, and their reign of terror came to an end.
The testimony of one poor lad, Edward Elliot by
name, only seventeen years of age, who seems to have
been their very unwilling tool, was extraordinary.
He asserted that a kind of ' witchcraft art ' was
practised by the community on those persons who
offended the Blacks and would not take their oath of
membership. Two such were blindfolded and buried
up to their chins in earth, while the freebooters danced
round them, barking like dogs. These unfortunates
were afterwards dismissed with a warning.

Elliot appears to have been terrified by threats
into accompanying the lawless crew on their raids,
but a forest keeper had been shot dead—actually
while the lad was in custody—and the authorities
were determined to show no mercy. Seven people
paid for that fatal shot with their lives, including the
wretched boy Elliot, whose sole desire seemed to be
to get away from his compellers. In these days he
would probably have been let off with a caution.

Granted that the punishment meted out to these
unhappy culprits was in general unconscionably harsh
and brutal, there is no doubt whatever that the
terrible conditions prevailing in the forest district
required dealing with by very strong measures. For
a long time knots of disbanded soldiers had collected
in parts of the dense jungle, where they built themselves huts, and whence they emerged to make war
on every one who could be preyed upon. The depre-
dations of the Waltham Blacks had been so flagrant

that a special act was passed in 1723, wherein it was ordained that ' whatever persons armed with offensive weapons, and having their faces blacked or otherwise disguised,' offending against the forest laws (indicated at length), ' should be deemed guilty of felony without benefit of clergy, and suffer pains of death as felons so convicted '.

For minor offences the stocks, the pillory, and the whipping-post were generally available, and there was sometimes an uncomfortable little lock-up cage, barely sufficient to hold more than a couple of offenders. One would scarcely have imagined that it would have been worth while to decorate any of these instruments of correction with carving, but our ancestors thought differently. The combined stocks and whipping-post at Waltham (now in the Abbey Church) is lavishly ornamented with strap-carving, and bears the date 1598—a far more highly embellished article than many ancient alms-boxes. The pillory, on the other hand, is a mean, weak-looking structure that seems to feel acutely the loss of its upper neck-board. Another fine whipping-post is, or used to be, at Good Easter, and excellent specimens of that grand old institution, the stocks, are at Doddinghurst, Roydon, and Havering-atte-Bower, all of which are on the borders of what was formerly the Great Essex Forest. When I last visited Great Canfield the remains of the stocks and whipping-post there were lying scattered about the ground, and seemed in the way of being lost or altogether destroyed.

I have it on the authority of Mr. Basil Fanshawe, who is referred to in another part of this work, that the combined stocks and whipping-post on the green at Havering-atte-Bower was presented by his great-grandfather, John Gascoyne Fanshawe (1746–1803).

Survivals of the uneasy little lock-ups which were provided in the seventeenth and eighteenth centuries for the temporary accommodation of local sinners may be seen at Witham, Roydon, and Tollesbury.

Stocks and Whipping Post,
Havering-atte-Bower

Some of these have actually been in use till the last seventy years or so.

Highwaymen whose necks were already forfeit cared little for such mild corrections as stocks or whipping-posts. Cavalry patrols on the high roads may have checked the activities of gangs of desperadoes, but they counted for little against those solitary free-lances who robbed for their own hand alone—and then bolted into the thickest parts of the

Fred Roe.

THE LOCK-UP, TOLLESBURY

maze.   Even to-day so dense is the growth off some of
the tracks of man and animal which dissect parts of
Epping Forest that unexpected things occasionally
come to light.   It is not many years ago that an
old man was discovered residing in a species of low
wigwam which he had constructed out of branches
and sacking.   This anchorite had been living there for
years without detection, and his only wish was to be
let alone and pass his time in squalid solitude.   Other
instances could be mentioned of more recent date,
but in every case the poverty-stricken squatters
were not allowed to remain.   Very differently circum-
stanced from these recluses was the celebrated John
Elwes, that miserly old gentleman, who had his good
points.   Theydon Hall, near Theydon Bois, was one
of his residences, but hardly any of the old building
survives.

That the forest teems with animal life need
scarcely be remarked ; its glades form a happy roam-
ing ground for a great many varieties, from the fallow
deer to the field mouse.   But surely one of the most
extraordinary instances of mass migration there
occurred in November 1927.   Recent floods at
Edmonton had made the neighbourhood uncomfortable for the local rats, and they had evidently planned
in a way peculiarly their own to move in force to
safer quarters.   It is said that they were guided by
a blind old leader, but at any rate their way was clear
to them.   A perfect horde of rodents, thousands upon
thousands in number, proceeded along the Lea Valley
road to Epping Forest ; a dark and evil-looking army,
which caused a clearance of pedestrians and dogs, as
well as cyclists from their path.

That there should be a scarcity of oaks of large

size in such an ancient woodland as that of Epping is
not to be wondered at. The material required for
framing up edifices like Paycocke's House at Coggeshall, the ' Red Lion ' Hotel at Colchester, and Queen
Elizabeth's Hunting Lodge at Chingford, must have
created gaps in forest land where the finest oaks used
to abound. During the centuries in which history
was making, the destruction of giant timber trees
must have outdistanced their slow growth in a most
alarming way. Brick eventually superseded wood in

Beamed ceiling in the ' Bull ' Inn, Halstead

the matter of domestic building ; but how the Wooden
Walls of England of Nelson's day would have been
replenished if an efficient substitute had not been
found for oak, it is difficult to surmise. Examine
any of the old Georgian ' perspective views ' of cities
and towns, which were so popular during the second
half of the eighteenth century, and what do we invariably see ? In the foreground is a gentleman in a
three-cornered hat and skirted coat, calling the attention of a lady, attired in a sacque dress, to the beauties

of a spired town in the middle distance. The land looks somewhat bare : there are very few trees about ; and a comparison of these plates with the same place from an approximate position at the present time will at once prove how much more wooded in a general way the country-side has become during the last hundred and fifty years. But this is through the increase of the softer and quicker-growing varieties of timber, for the giant British oaks, which took anything from five hundred to a thousand years to reach their prime, have mostly disappeared for ever.

Dickens describes an outing in Epping Forest in his amusing article, ' The Young Ladies' Young Gentleman,' in which he speaks of the trip being made in ' four glass coaches, each with a trifling company of six or eight inside, and a little boy belonging to the projectors on the box '. Further on he mentions that : ' We dined rather more comfortably than people do under such circumstances, nothing having been left behind but the corkscrew and the bread.'

No finer stalking-ground for training the intelligence of Boy Scouts can be found than the forest and its borders. This fact must have been recognized by Mr. W. F. de Bois Maclaren, who in 1919 purchased and presented to the Boy Scouts' Association, as a training centre, the old hunting lodge at Gillwell Park, on the Sewardstone border of the forest. Occasionally one comes across these sons of Britain in unexpected places, carrying out their jobs with quick understanding. But the forest is more inscrutable when the patrols have gone home, when the deer roam at dusk, and the moths flit among the tree boles. Then, it is said, the ghost of Gillwell Park walks abroad, and believers in the wraith are not wanting.

CHAPTER XVII

OLD CUSTOMS AND SUPERSTITIONS

WITCHCRAFT is said to be still performed in Essex. It may be, but I have never yet come across any one who practised the 'curious arts', though I have met plenty of simple souls who believed in such things. There are some who hold that Matthew Hopkins, the great witch-finder (who was a native of Manningtree), did not succeed in extirpating the sect altogether, for was he not made to suffer from a dose of his own fatal medicine, before he could complete the task ? But of ancient superstitious customs a good many linger among country-folk in the outlying parts of Essex. Injuries inflicted by a nail, knife, or pin are supposed to be cured by heating the offending article in the flame of a candle. Some believers in this remedy even go so far as to extend it to animals. Simple specifics like this do not require the superintendence of such sage folk as Cunning Murrell, a Hadleigh character, who died in 1856 ; but time after time accounts crop up of small farmers whose cattle are suspected of being bewitched, whereupon their owners have recourse to the 'wise woman' to heal them. More curious still is the fact that the means employed have not unfrequently been reported as turning out successful.

But what about the wretched suspects of witchcraft ? Mostly there was no evidence whatever against them, the dislike engendered by a squint, a lowering expression, or possibly by some curious impediment in their speech being quite sufficient cause for persecution. So late as 1863 a case of supposed witchcraft occurred at Castle Hedingham, which reads for all the world like an extract from some romance

The ' Four Want Way ', Larkin's Corner, Orsett

of the eighteenth century rather than actual reality. A woman of the village afflicted with rheumatic pains imagined that a spell must have been cast over her by a harmless old man who had settled in the neighbourhood. That the suspected person was ' a foreigner ' was, to some, sufficient evidence in itself, but in addition to this disadvantage the man was deaf and dumb, and could only make himself understood with difficulty. Relatives and friends of the sickly woman formed themselves into a sort of council of justice, and beat and ill-used the old fellow to such an extent that his death ensued. It does not appear, however, that the distressed woman derived any benefit from this drastic behaviour on her behalf. There have been similar instances in quite recent years, though not attended with fatal results.

According to the philosophy of John Wellington Wells, sixpenny blessings are less in demand than penny curses, but beneficent formulas have been carried out—and still are—though perhaps they are now retained more as survivals of ancient customs than from any belief in their efficacy. In October 1928, two experimental cottages were opened at Thorpe-le-Soken, celebrated for its association with Kitty Cannom. The tenements had been built by the Tendring Rural Council, and the ground on which they stood had been generously presented by Lady Byng, who on opening the cottages threw bread and coal across their thresholds into the living-rooms as a symbol that the occupants should never want food or fire.

Of the survival, or revival, of the ceremony of the Flitch at Dunmow, little need be said except that it is a travesty of its former self. The account of how various couples have, so to speak, saved their bacon, must be looked for elsewhere. When last heard of that mysterious midnight ritual known as the ' Lawless ', or ' Whispering Court ', held at Rayleigh and Rochford, seemed to be treated in much the same spirit. Both of these observances appear to have lost their original significances.

I am afraid that among the extinctions which have taken place during the last thirty years or so

THE BLACKSMITH OF KELVEDON

must be reckoned the old-fashioned harvest home feasts, when could be heard such ditties as :

> ' Singing songs of high down derry.
> Drinking ale as brown as berry.
> To drown dull care
> We'll drink small beer,
> To the health of our Harvest Home.'

or :

> ' When the bee be on the turmut top,
> And I goes turmuts hoeing.'

In happier days for agriculture such mighty gotchs as are preserved at Halstead and Colchester Castle were passed round from hand to hand, filled with home-brewed ale to stimulate the choruses.

At Berden on the north-west border of Essex the ancient ceremony of electing a boy bishop has been revived. The church is dedicated to St. Nicholas, the patron saint of children, and the election takes place on 6th of December (the Saint's festival), when the little ' Nicholas ' is properly vested and processes about the parish with his ' clerks '. The ceremony at Berden is a modification of the original custom, when it was taken so seriously that, among other rights, in the event of the boy bishop dying during his prelacy the proper funeral honours of a pontiff were accorded him. In the nave of Salisbury Cathedral a slab, incised with the miniature figure in episcopal vestments, is *said* to represent an instance of this observance.

The song of the anvil grows fainter in Essex. The art of the old-time village craftsman in iron practically vanished with the growth of mass production in Birmingham, and the blacksmith's cunning in shaping horseshoes and tyres is now but little in request. Many of the ancient forges are cold. The quaint timber smithy on Leigh Hill has retired from that class of business ; its fires are out for ever, and the aged proprietor has taken to selling books and furniture. Of that cheery giant specimen of his class at Kelvedon—pictured by me—I have pleasant recollections, and hope his craft has not suffered so that he has been driven to other pursuits, in face of those unsightly garages of modern requirements.

But a short decade and the thatcher's craft will surely be extinct in Essex. Practisers of this ancient industry grow fewer in numbers, co-incident with the roofs they have to repair, and these diligent folk often have to travel wide distances to do their work. To renew the roof of a cottage at Hanwell in 1928 (one of the few thatched houses remaining in the London area), a reed thatcher had to be brought all the way from the New Forest. The call for such elaborate thatching as may be seen at Stifford does not exist in sufficient quantities nowadays to encourage apprenticeship to the craft. Among the curiosities of our small country towns are frequently reckoned some outlying thatched cottages whose very existence would have been unnoticed a few years ago. If you ever see these roofs being renovated, the workman is invariably an ancient of days, picturesque and fustian-clad. Below in the village street the juvenile population watches, gaping. For the man is almost a bygone. And with the passing of the thatcher another of our old English personalities will have disappeared for ever.

INDEX

Printed in Great Britain by
Butler & Tanner Ltd.,
Frome and London